MY LIFE IN THE FURNACE

Panayotis Tranoulis was born in Aigion, and his family moved to Athens when he was two years old.

As a seven-year old, instead of attending school, he was forced to work in a furnace to help support his family, following his father's death. At twelve, he realized that he would never be able to attend school, and he decided to teach himself to read at night.

He has published four critically and commercially acclaimed books. His first book, *Keratohori* was published in Greece in 1973. It has been translated and published in Russia and Hungary. It has also been translated in English, German and Italian and it is currently being translated into Chinese.

His work has appeared on the Greek National Public Radio, narrated in thirteen episodes by renowned actor Kostas Kazakos.

PANAYOTIS TRANOULIS

MY LIFE IN THE FURNACE

KERATOHORI

Translated by
Marjorie Chambers

Edited by
C. Capri-Karka

ΡΕLLΔ
Pella Publishing Company, Inc.
New York, NY 10018-6401
2005

MY LIFE IN THE FURNACE
Keratohori

© Copyright 2005
by
PANAYOTIS TRANOULIS

Library of Congress Control Number 2005906995

ISBN: 0918618916

COVER DESIGN BY: *Vivian Zhang*

PRINTED IN THE UNITED STATES OF AMERICA
BY
ATHENS PRINTING COMPANY
337 West 36th Street
New York, NY 10018-6401

ACKNOWLEDGEMENTS

I wish to express my grateful thanks to Roya Liakopoúlou-Hughes who gave generously of her time when consulted, also to Peter and Tony Minter of the Bulmer Brick and Tile Company Ltd.,* Suffolk, England, who provided valuable information. I am also indebted to the author, Panayótis Tranoúlis.

---

*The Bulmer Brick and Tile Company Ltd. in Suffolk, England makes hand-made bricks by following strictly traditional methods. The bricks are purpose made for every order, often for restoration work, notably for Hampton Court Palace and more recently for St. Pancras Station, London. The site has been used for brick-making, probably continuously, from 1450 until the present day.

TRANSLATOR'S NOTE

The Greek accent which I have used in proper names indicates where the word is stressed.

FOREWORD

VASÍLIS RÓTAS AND VOÚLAS DAMIANÁKOU
FOR THE FIRST EDITION (1973)

At one time a teacher in a "proper" school, attended by children of "proper" parents who belonged to the "proper" social class, would set the pupils to write an "essay of ideas" on the very "proper" social theme "A poor family". One of the pupils wrote:

"Once there was a very poor family. The father was very poor. The mother was very poor; the children were very poor; their nanny was very poor; the cook was very poor; the chauffeur was very poor; the gardener was very poor . . ."

The child who wrote the essay on poverty knew only the word and only on hearsay. He didn't know either its nature or its attributes. He didn't even know what part of speech it was.

Perhaps he thought that poverty was something well-known since the teacher had set them this subject, or perhaps that it was very common, good or bad, or, it was something out of a fairy-tale and so he registered his ignorance in the manner of a fairy-tale—as if to say: "Once upon a time there was a very good family. The father was very good" . . . etc.

Panayótis Tranoúlis's "Keratohóri" is also, in a way, an "essay" on the same subject, written by a man who personally studied in the school of poverty and only in that school.

As for state or private schools Tranoúlis had only heard of them and never crossed their thresholds.

At the age of six or seven, and fatherless, the cruel hand of necessity flung Tranoúlis, without any provisions, into the sea of the harsh struggle for life, leaving him to swim or sink.

Of course children in this category, the orphans and the extremely poor, who never went to any school, also have their names written down in some records, in municipal rolls as male or female.

But it would be a mistake for one to believe that because our society has their names on its account books it owes them anything. No, the plight of these children is not considered to be a social matter that is worth anyone being debited with. Not even as the soldier is debited with various pieces of military equipment.

If these children are lost no one will be held accountable for their loss and no one, apart from their mother, if they have any, will look for them, if they are killed.

So then what do the account books signify?

That the children of the poor should be born burdened from father to son with social parasitism, with having to observe the laws . . . serve their country . . . do their duty.

Poverty is a terrible illness that makes people who suffer from it outcasts of society, as if they themselves were responsible for their condition.

And no one is concerned with the cure for it. The only

medicine, as the doctor would say, is for the organism to weather it.

For those who manage, under their own steam, to escape from poverty, our society hastens to open its doors and welcome them as remarkable members of it, the chosen, sometimes the elite, and all clients of the Department of Inland Revenue.

Panayótis Tranoúlis turned out to be one of the lucky ones.

He conquered illness, hunger, appalling conditions, harsh and inhuman work. He didn't sink as did so many in the underworld. On the contrary, he managed to get out onto dry land, carrying with him treasures, among which the first offering was "Keratohóri".

Fate determined Tranoúlis's lot, pitied him and hung a talisman around his neck. It planted in his heart the sacred passion of the creator.

And it is this passion, this sacred flame which helped him, not only to emerge victorious from the trials of poverty and being fatherless, but to give us, with "Keratohóri" the chronicle of these experiences.

It was this passion which made him impose a more difficult duty upon himself in addition to that which dreadful necessity imposed on him—namely, to learn reading and writing, not only to come into contact and become acquainted with the great wide world which was being denied him, but also to describe his life of poverty and hard labour with the workers and the bosses, and with children who never went to school, who worked far beyond their physical strength, who never knew a caress, but only threats and blows on the head, and over whom the master moulders had "almost divine power".

He learned to read and write in order to tell us about strikes, strike-breakers, spies, and idealists, and about the first steps towards trade-unionism in our country.

The sacred flame of the artist made Tranoúlis discover charms and treasures in his deprived and joyless life, and he set himself to hoard the kind words of old Apostólis, the humility of Nikólas, the unique caress from an aunt, the singing of Goldfinch, the chatter of a little girl.

The sacred flame of the creator made him see that out of the harshness and the ill-treatment came drops of tenderness; that smiles blossomed, words showered compassion and looks shone with love. It enabled him to regard as his relative even Kotsíkos who crippled him with the moulder's "strike" . . .

It is this flame which made him see that beyond the mud-brick huts and the cruelty, beyond "Keratohóri" with all the flowers of evil that bloomed in it, there were birds that sang, the sun that shone, and the sea that mirrored the endless sky. There were mountains, forests, flowers. There was song.

In "Keratohóri" there are no adornments, no figures of speech.

In simple and one would even say spare language, whose descriptive capability isn't always enough to clothe his meanings—which here and there suddenly appear as do the people in the life that he describes—Tranoúlis manages to set before us a whole area of human life in all its wretchedness, in conditions so harsh and inhuman that they would shame our society if it had the grace to feel shame.

The scenes he describes are so vivid and have such immediacy that the reader's participation in them becomes so intense and all-embracing it creates in him the feeling that he himself, without any intermediary, is living this nightmare life.

Reading "Keratohóri" you realise that beyond the misery your mind comprehends is another that it doesn't comprehend, that beyond the greatest poverty there is an even greater.

Tranoúlis didn't begin life even on the lowest rung of the ladder. For him it began from out of the clay of the furnace, from out of the mud that the flood left in the place where formerly the mud huts sheltered the life that he describes.

He began life from the dark depths of the underworld: "Keratohóri" is a yard-stick that measures the gap of social injustice and inequality.

Very few such images of life have been given us.

Here people are not play-acting; they are not telling sad stories in order to be pitied, rather, in the telling of them it's as if they are putting their hands to their throats and choking in order to persuade philanthropic society that they really are in distress.

This book, which is a series of tragic peaks, expresses great suffering, but nowhere are there bewailings, superfluous words or histrionics. On the contrary there is understanding, high principles, forgiveness, courage, and even humour which is also one of the marks of true poetry.

1950. Workers at the furnace in Nea Makri, Attikis. Panayotis Tranoulis is second from the right.

MY LIFE IN
THE FURNACE

It is hard to write down all I saw and lived through.
There are many things I cannot bear to tell.
I write the things that leave me heart to breathe.

MY LIFE IN THE FURNACE

Immediately after my father's death, my mother took me and my brother, Alékos to work in the brick furnace belonging to Pandelís Krápas. Here, our father had worn out what was left of the strength in his hands. That first morning my mother took us to ask for work, we stood for a long time and no one came near us. I saw that my mother was in despair and I couldn't help myself; the tears ran out of my eyes. After a while a small man, slightly bow-legged approached us. I heard later that he was called Manólis and was nicknamed Kopsós. He greeted my mother with respect. "Good-day, Mrs Mítsaina."

"Good-day," replied my mother, deeply touched. "I can see they're young for this work," she went on, "but their father has just died."

"I know, I know," replied Kopsós, and took us by the hand, saying to my mother, "Leave the children and I'll fit them in somewhere."

"A thousand blessings on you, a thousand blessings," cried my mother, ready to weep. She went quickly away, as if to prevent her tears falling in front of Kopsós. As he was taking us off with him he said sadly, in a whisper: "The father has died and they're bringing the children to carry on the family slavery."

The moulders who took us on as apprentices were friends of my father. They had worked for years together. Sometimes they would say: "He was a good father, a kind-hearted man ...." I was moved that they spoke with respect for my father's memory. I was so grateful to them I wanted to fall at their feet so that they could walk over me. I thought, "How wonderful it is to be good," and I felt like crying. However, I still have some bitter feelings about those worthy people. While my father had only recently died they made me sing and dance for their amusement. Whenever they forced me do this, in the evening when I went home, I was ashamed to look my mother and sisters in the face. When we first went to the furnace looking for work, a tall man from the island of Thermiá, an uncle of the boss, as soon as he saw us, started onto us in a snarling voice: "What d'*you* want here?"

"They're Mítsos Tranoúlis's family," somebody butted in. He looked at us closely, "Aah! You're Mítsos Tranoúlis's family?" he said in a much softer tone. This sudden softening in his attitude towards us showed that he thought my father was a person worthy of respect and I took to him. But I realised at once that our lives in this place would be harsh and cruel.

The moulders had near divine power over us. They beat us severely for the slightest thing. No one had the right to speak to them about anything they did to us apprentices. It was as if this was an unwritten law and they regarded it as their sacred right.

Our homes were near the furnace and any apprentice who was being given a thrashing could be heard in the whole neighbourhood. From the cries of each of us our mothers knew which one they were beating. Occasionally, somebody's mother would arrive in tears. She would wipe the blood from his face and whisper to him: "Why don't you do what you're told, child? What did you do to make him butcher you like this? Watch out or he'll kill you some time."

The child's mother would say nothing to the moulder. She knew what the reply would be: "Take him home, missus" and that meant home to die of hunger. When the mother was instructing her unfortunate child she was careful to let the moulder hear that she was on his side and not on her son's so that she could keep the boy at work.

One time Mihaloú, a woman from Máni, whose son Dikaíos was being beaten, arrived with a piece of wood in her hand. She took a swipe at the moulder, Theodósis and cut his lip. The moulder saw her running up to him and didn't try to defend himself. One of the other moulders said: "He would not have imagined that Mihaloú would dare to hit him, or that he would be ashamed to show cowardice in front of a woman."

Mihaloú was the only woman who ever hit a moulder. She took her child and left. Next morning back came Mihaloú to the furnace with her son. "Forgive me moulder. May good fortune shine on your family and may your marriage be blessed. I have five young children and my husband is in hospital. We're waiting to eat bread from this one's wage," whimpered Mihaloú, pointing to her son who was so frail he had to force himself to stand upright. Dikaíos was dark-haired. His thin face was deathly pale, which made you doubt if the child was fit for this kind of work, and he didn't look as if he had the courage to say it; not a word could fall from his dry lips. "Go away from me. I don't want to see you," said the moulder, and gave her a push, but without malice. "It's your fault that your children are lazy and disobedient. You gave them the boldness to be like that and then they can't be made to do anything."

"Forgive me moulder. I was in the wrong. I could see that myself. I was so grieved about it, I wept and said, 'He's a good man. I'll beg him to forgive me.' What is a poor woman to do? Am I not a mother too?" Clasping her hands together she made a pleading gesture which showed how distressed she was. When the moulder pushed her Mihaloú swayed as if she were going to fall. Petrán, one of the moulders, commented: "Mihaloú did it on purpose. She acted frail and weak when Theodósis pushed her so that he might feel sorry for her and she would achieve something with that, as well as with her very sad face."

Theodósis didn't seem to be a stubborn man, but he stood by his refusal to the end.

A few days later Mihaloú came again. She begged the moulder, falling at his feet and weeping. He refused her as he had done the first time. A worker called Pávlos, when he saw Mihaloú leaving, said: "Theodósis will never forgive her. When he sees her she'll remind him of the blow." Someone else added: "The scar on Theodósis' lip will be a reminder that anyone who doesn't respect the weak and tramples over them won't get away with it. His punishment will come from somewhere."

The boss kept away from interfering in such matters. He just wanted his quota of bricks, and hadn't spoken to the moulders about the incident. They kept silent about it as if they had an unwritten agreement. One day he made a remark to the moulder, Stámos: "You go too far. I see that you beat the children as if they were animals. You've declared guerrilla rule in here."

After he said this the boss went away quickly, indicating that he didn't want to waste time on further comment.

Stámos was a mild man. He didn't beat the children, nor did he scold them. Pisadákis, a young moulder said: "You think the boss said this out of pity for the children? He came to Stámos like that to remind us that he exists."

Stámos didn't appear to be angry at the boss's remark. After a moment or two he stopped slicing bricks and smoked a cigarette at his place in front of the bench, looking thoughtful. Then he showed that he couldn't put up with an insult from the boss that they weren't accustomed to. He threw off his apron, washed himself, got dressed, and went on his way.

Stámos was a man in dire need. He had many children, as had almost all the moulders. He used to talk about his poverty, and when he said goodbye to us, I wept. I wanted to fall at his feet and beg him to stay, but I thought better of it. What he did was a question of dignity and the moulders understood and respected that. When he was walking away I felt as if a part of me had gone. Stámos was the first moulder I worked with and he helped me to endure the harsh rules that governed our lives in the furnace. When Kopsós presented me to the moulders, nobody wanted to take me on.

"How could you produce anything with this child? What size of mould could *he* manage?" said Theodósis first, and the others followed one by one, voicing their objections.

"Come here," Kopsós called to me. I went up to him. He took me by the hand and brought me through rows of bricks stacked up. He walked quickly muttering, "Scoundrels! Doesn't an orphan have to live? Don't they think what fate could befall their own children?" While he led me along he took a good look at me as if he were weighing up whether or not I was capable of working. I could see his lips tighten. I understood from this expression that he wasn't satisfied and I felt disheartened and dismayed. We stopped in front of a moulder, a tall dark man.

"Look here, Stámos, will *you* take him on. You'd be doing an act of charity," said Kopsós, and his voice broke. You would have thought he was going to weep, but when I heard him talk like that I couldn't help myself and began to cry.

"So be it," replied Stámos, and smiling, he stretched out his arms to me. I could see that in this place it depended on someone's good will whether you lived, or died of hunger, and I said to myself that I would never forget Stámos; I'd be grateful to him as long as I lived. By his example, it was as if he had put a sacred light into me to remind me always to do good.

Each moulder had three apprentices to bring him the moulds. Kopsós took the oldest boy away from Stámos's bench and replaced him with me and brought him to do other work that I couldn't do. When Kopsós went off the moulder scrutinized me and said: "Look what we've come to, my friend! Ruining our lives from the first steps we take. They've brought a mere chit of a child to work who should be going to school. He'll be as illiterate as a blind man. He'll never be able to learn anything. What sort of man will he be? How will he manage this heavy work? He'll be worn to a shadow."

It was as if the moulder had struck me on the head with this crushing truth. He didn't consider that his words, which cruelly revealed to me that my life was being destroyed, might make me grieve. In the evening, when I went to bed his words came back to me and I began to cry.

When Kopsós first took me to Stámos, the other boys, who would be working with me, looked at me with animosity. One of them, annoyed at the sight of me, said: "They didn't bring his cradle with him," and the "feeder", a big boy who carried clay in a wheel-barrow to the moulding bench and passed lumps of it to the moulder, also looked at me with hostility, and murmured: "He's a snotty child for this kind of work."

I was frightened when I heard this. I feared that the moulder might change his mind and not keep me. As I realised eventually, I *was* too young. I wasn't at all fit for this work and I was causing harm to them. When one of the three children wasn't in time with the mould he held up the work, and the moulders were behind with production, and so were late going home.

When Stámos left, our bench was without a moulder. The boss sent Kopsós, who was his cousin and he also had the authority that might persuade the moulder to return; Stámos was foreman at the kiln, well known in all the furnaces.

Everyone held him in respect and his word carried a lot of weight. Kopsós didn't succeed in persuading Stámos to return, and the boss looked regretful. A moulder called Aléxis Skamángas, who was an artist at our kind of work, said about the boss, Krápas, "What does he want, interfering with us? Isn't the job done? Is it us who beat the children or is it he? *He* beats them with our hands. As if we're not sorry for them? I look at them and pity them from my heart. We drive them hard. From the morning we push them to the limits; we work them to death. They're young children. They get tired, and we thrash them on top of that."

He took a deep breath and went on: "But look how the boss demands ten thousand bricks a day from each bench. In other furnaces they produce nine. Who beats the children then? We or the boss? He beats them with our hands." He looked very moved, ready to cry. "Who would Aléxis Skamángas be going to cry for? Just for the children or for himself too?" said Theodósis, who would have seen clearly that Skamángas too was like all of us, a victim who suffered; at such moments, we suffer and cry, young and old. If I hadn't heard Skamángas talking like this I wouldn't have believed it—he, the fierce-looking one, who beat the children more barbarously than the other moulders, was hiding a compassionate heart.

When we finished producing the ten thousand bricks sometimes a small piece of clay would be left over. We called this piece the "tamboúra".[1] The boss wanted us to cut bricks

---

[1] "*tamboúra*"—"the piece [of clay] left over". According to the author this word bears no relation to anything.

from it after we had finished producing our quota, and without payment. Then the moulder would say to us: "Listen here, little bastards, we're not cutting bricks from the "tamboúra". And if the boss asks why I've left it, I'll tell him you got tired and started crying. Agreed? Remember, or else!" In the end they held the threat over our young heads so that none of us ever knew if the required number of bricks was made or not.

After the moulder there was the "feeder". He hadn't the right to beat us, the mould carriers. That was strictly forbidden by the moulder. But whenever there was a "tamboúra" left over and the moulder warned us about what he would say to the boss, and frightened us with the threat "Remember, or else!", then the "feeder" would show us his huge paw and say sarcastically: "Look what's waiting for you." And when we didn't manage to prove to the boss that it was because of us that the "tamboúra" wasn't cut into bricks, the moulder let him give us a slap too.

The work at the bench was carried out extremely quickly. The moulder filled the moulds like a machine and we three youngsters took them and ran to the drying ground as fast as we could to empty them and catch up with the moulder. If a brick stuck in the mould and kept us back, or one of us could not run fast enough to keep up, then the moulder became furious, blaspheming and cursing our families, and we felt the weight of his big, muddy hand wherever it happened to fall on us—on the face, the head, the back, the neck!

The blows on the neck that rained down on us all day, covered our hair and neck with clay. When it dried, hair and neck became one, and as we tried to turn our heads, we couldn't. When we turned we were as rigid as a wolf, and when we bent, our heads hurt, as if someone was pulling our hair back.

The sun would be burning hot in the oppressive summer. We would run with as much strength as we could muster. The sweat poured from us and the moulder's hand fell on us like the carter's whip on his exhausted little horse.

I was younger than all the other children. In the evening, when we got out of work, there was no limit to my tiredness. I was completely exhausted. I would fall unconscious into a hole filled with sand which we took to coat the moulds. The oldest boys, to amuse themselves, would sometimes open a hole in the sand and drag me in. They would cover me with it, leaving only my head uncovered. Then they would make fun of me and when they got tired of laughing they would dig me out and tumble me around like something lifeless. I was so tired that I felt as if I were dead.

One time they forgot to dig me out. I fell asleep buried like that. I hadn't the strength to get myself out. When I awoke the stars had come out. Every noise that came to my ears frightened me. I was seized with fear that a dog would come and eat me, or some imaginary wild beast would appear, or a ghost like the ones they talked about that people young and old had seen.

While I was in the throes of my anguish my mother came weeping with two boys from the neighbourhood and they dug me out.

FAMILY

Thodorís, at twenty years old, was the eldest of my mother's children. After my father's funeral he left home. He went and found work far away from us, in a brick furnace at Ierá Eliá (the Sacred Olive Tree) and he forgot us. A woman neighbour, discussing him with my mother said: "Mrs Mítsaina, he's like somebody whose wife has died. They have no children and he immediately cuts all ties with her family."

My second brother, Yánnis, almost eighteen, kept a mistress, a woman of the streets, and he too left home after Thodorís.

They were both skilled moulders and earned a good wage. Yánnis worked in a furnace further away from us and we used to get news of him. They gave him the nickname, Nipyánnis because he had a passion for setting up nets to catch birds and then he would nip them on the neck with his nail and kill them. One day Aléxis Skamángas said maliciously: "Have you heard the news? His lady-love has given him the medal."

I didn't know then what "medal" was. Later I found out that it was a venereal disease. There were very many young people crowded into that neighbourhood and they lived in degradation and corruption.

After Yánnis came, my sister Athanasía, sixteen years old, kind and hard-working. The clothes she wore were plain and of poor quality, but they were always spotlessly clean and carefully ironed. My other sister, Eléni was fourteen. She was simple and gullible, with the innocence of a child, almost naïve. She loved fantastic stories and could be absorbed for hours hearing about the lives of the saints. Unconcerned about her appearance, anything new she wore would quickly become shabby on her and have to be patched. The same with her shoes; she wore them in such a way that she twisted them and the stitching came apart. She would go about barefoot in the neighbourhood to save her shoes being ruined.

My sisters worked in Yannoukákis's tobacco factory near Lávrion Station, and our house was further down from Rouf Barracks. It was four or five kilometres to the factory, and they went there and back on foot. They left in the morning when it was dark and returned in the evening when it was pitch-black. When it rained my mother would go to meet them with a piece of oilcloth to try to protect them from the rain, but they always came in soaking wet. Mrs Stéfaina said once about my mother: "Mítsaina doesn't save the girls from getting wet. But she's there when they need her."

Next to Eléni was Alékos, nine years old and very delicate. Now and then he lisped a bit and so he was teased. One day, when it was cold, he was walking along hunched up. Pisadákis, the great tease of the neighbourhood said to him: "Hey, Alékos, why are you *mazeménos* (hunched up)? Are you cold?"

"No," replied my brother, "I'm *mathiméno* (used to it)."

Thereafter Pisadákis called him *Masiméno* (mumbler) and when he was of mature age he was still called *Masiméno*.

I was born after Alékos and after me there was another sister, Vangelítsa. Last in the family came Manólis about two years old. My mother continued to breast feed him because she had nothing more to give him to eat.

From somewhere the girls found out the whereabouts of my brother, Thodorís who had disappeared. They went to the place where he was living and found him. He beat them and threw them out. On the evening when we had in the house the boiled wheat for my father's memorial service, forty days after his death, we were wakened at midnight by musical instruments being played in horse-cabs, and drunken voices singing.

"Hey, Athanasía, it's that good-for-nothing Thodorís, it's *his* voice," said my mother to my big sister. Exasperated, she strained her ear to listen. She stayed for a while like that. Then slowly the exasperation on her face seemed to fade away and there remained only the longing to hear that voice that she missed and grieved for. She seemed to be forgiving him, no matter how deeply he had wounded her tormented mother's heart. Before we got back to sleep a knock was heard on our door. "Coming," my mother called out and jumped up. She put on her dressing-gown and hastily opened the door as if she was expecting something good to come to us. The beautiful dream perhaps that every poor person has, the dream that is his only hope and consolation.

"Good evening, neighbour," came the voice of Mítraina, who kept goats. Her large herd used to bleat all the time and soil even more the dirty alley of our poor neighbourhood. Small and frail, and as always, drunk as a fiddler, she came in and put a plate of doughnuts on the table. She turned to my mother and said: "This evening Mrs Mítsaina, we're going to be related by marriage. Your son Thodorís is getting engaged to my sister, Vasilikí, and I've come to invite you to be with us."

My mother's head jerked back, as if she had been given a hard blow. Her eyes filled with tears and she spoke slowly and softly, in a strangled voice: "I don't have a son called Thodorís."

"Come now Mrs Mítsaina, don't be like that. You're not a bad person. I thought you'd be happy for us to become related. The young people are to be married. We're not marrying them ourselves, are we? Say 'yes' from your heart. Give him your blessing and get ready and we'll go."

Mítraina thought of us as being very much beneath her which was why she told my mother she should be happy that their families were going to be connected. She had two hovels surrounded by a fence of mud bricks. One had two rooms that were barely habitable and the other was kept for the goats. Her husband Mítrou's work was with the goats; the family was busy with them all day. They smelt of manure and goats, living an animal-like life among the goats, but they were able to eat.

"It's not for me to say 'yes'. Let him ask for that from his father," said my mother, lifting the sheet of paper that covered the dish with the boiled wheat.

In the middle of the dish there was a cross made with

raisins and at the sides my father's name spelled out with little silver-coated sugar almonds. "Here he is. Let him come and ask him. Is he ashamed or afraid?" said my mother and burst into sobs.

Mrs Mítraina left with bowed head.

They were carousing with music and songs at the engagement party. Two or three houses separated us from them and we could hear them as if they were in our yard. My mother didn't go back to bed. She sat on the chair at the table, with our little lamp dimmed. She was huddled into a ball and was crying.

Suddenly we heard a terrible noise and our little door opened with a bang, nearly falling off its hinges. Thodorís rushed in, swooped on our mother and slapped her hard on the face several times. Crying and shouting, "Mom, mom," we children tried to stop him.

Thodorís, having vented his anger by slapping her, began to revile our poor mother who was stunned with the blows: "Scoundrel, scamp, witch, good-for-nothing, beggar, louse! We do you the honour of inviting you and you insult the lady of the house."

With this sudden assault my mother didn't have time to say a word. Dazed, she looked at Thodorís, her hair unbraided and tousled. Blood was running from her nostrils and mouth. She wiped it with the back of her hand, looked at it with surprise and said to Thodorís who was reviling her, beside himself with anger: "I spit on you. Are you not ashamed" and instead of saliva, he was spattered with blood. He flew at our mother again, even more enraged, beating her wherever his hand happened to fall, as if he would kill her. We tried to stop him again, crying and shrieking "Mom, mom." We got entangled around her trying to save her, and he beat us and flung us off like rubbish.

My sister Eléni went out to the yard and shouted: "Help, help. He's killing us!"

The house and the yard filled with people. My mother was lying unconscious. The women were around her, trying to revive her. Noákaina, who acted as midwife in the neighbourhood and whose opinion counted, said in a frightened voice: "She is not going to live. The criminal has killed her. We must get her to the hospital quick!"

Hrístaina, a white-haired woman who never spoke much, and who used to help us all, said: "We must wash her first or she'll choke with the blood. He's even broken her teeth!"

The men had gathered round Thodorís. They swore at him and spat at him in disgust: "Shame on you, coward, scoundrel, beast!"

A tall, sturdy man, Yorghákis Mariólis, who had spent years in prison for murder and whom everyone in the neighbourhood feared, leapt forward to get hold of him, shouting fiercely: "Stay there you scoundrel. I'll hang your guts round your neck!"

He didn't manage to lay hands on him. The others came between them and helped him to escape.

They took my mother to Evangelismós hospital. I didn't know where Evangelismós was but I knew the name. Whenever I heard it I would be grieved and sometimes I would cry. My father had been ill there for a time and then they brought him back dead to the house. They took out the door of our house, set up some chairs as stands and put him on top. Tzanís, a strong workman from Naxos, found some planks from packing cases in the neighbourhood and made a coffin. Such was our fate there—to make coffins for one another. When anyone asking after a sick person said: "How goes his health?" the other would reply jokingly: "How do you think it's going?. They're ready to make his coffin." Whenever I heard this tragic joke, it would stir my blood.

With the death of my father there was no laughter and singing in the house for years. As I never stopped singing, even in my sleep, this affected me deeply; I seemed to be growing old inside. Sometimes I couldn't keep silent. I would hum something like a dirge, without words, just sad thoughts about my joyless young life.

After some days they brought my mother back from the hospital, her face and head swathed in bandages. It was in my mother's nature to talk very little. When she came back from the hospital you would have thought she had become dumb.

Whenever I saw her she would be in floods of tears. She was not crying only because of the wounds, but also from sorrow that her own son had beaten her, I heard her say to Mrs Hrístaina.

The family of Panayotis Tranoulis.

KERATOHORI

K eratohóri was an isolated hollow, with forty or fifty houses. In the rare flooding disasters that occurred, the water would make holes in the mud-brick walls and pour into the houses.

The name I first heard of for this neighbourhood of hovels was Platyfréa.[1] Eventually people from Máni[2] swelled the number of its inhabitants and it was then called Maniátika. Then later on, one morning, when a pair of sheep's horns[3] was found hanging on a door they called the neighbourhood, Keratohóri.[4]

In the course of time women of ill fame came to settle in Keratohóri. They brought with them some suspicious individuals, introducing them as their husbands. From time to time these husbands disappeared and were replaced by cousins and uncles, and other such relatives, of the same suspect appearance as the first lot.

---

[1]*Platyfréa* means broad hollow.

[2]The Máni area in the south-west Peloponnese covers the last thirty miles of the Taygetus mountain as far as Cape Mátapan. The population is distributed in the mountain villages.

[3]"A pair of sheep's horns"—*éna zevghári kérata* was hung on a man's door by someone, implying that his wife has been unfaithful to him.

[4]*Keratohóri* means the place of the horns.

Thanks to these noteworthy persons, whose numbers increased significantly, Keratohóri developed as a thriving commercial centre. It began with women, hashish, morphine, and all kinds of drugs, and progressed to local fabrics, textiles, men's suits, women's clothes, furs, watches, shoes, and jewellery that had been stolen from big shops and houses in Athens.

Cards, dice, and pitch-and-toss for the children had become an almost regular occupation. The dominant figure in this underworld was Antónis Papaconstantínou. He frequently took a share of the winnings at cards and dice by bullying the players. He didn't take anything from the pitch-and-toss game that the children played.

These he left alone. "The children will be my future customers," he used to boast.

Antónis was born in Keratohóri, son of Sotíris, a small, old man, a sly native of Épirus. Sotíris also had a younger son, Níkos who showed great zeal in his efforts to resemble his brother. He was older than me. We worked for the same moulder. He found it hard to get up in time in the morning to go to work. I used to call at his house and take him with me. Whenever he couldn't be bothered going he would begin to think up some illness. One time he put into action his plan to avoid work, with the excuse of a sore leg; the evening before, he bandaged his leg and pretended to limp. Next morning, when I woke him, he came out limping with the bandaged leg.

"I'm not coming," he told me, "My leg's sore," and he screwed up his face as if he were in pain.

His mother, a skinny, hunchbacked woman, put her thin little face out the door and backed him up: "The wee soul didn't sleep a wink all night with the pain."

Then his father, Sotíris came out and said: "What's the matter Níko? Aren't you going to work today?"

Níkos, mumbled: "Look, my leg . . ." and glanced at his mother, who was listening, as if begging her to support him.

"So, you won't be able to work? Does it hurt so much?" Sotíris asked him slyly again.

"I can't work. It hurts," replied Níkos in a strained voice, and he limped two or three steps to the door and hid himself away in the house. It looked as if he had got away with it.

"Wait a minute," his father said to me. "You're going to have a laugh! Last night, while he was sleeping I took the bandage off one leg and put it on the other, without him knowing."

I was amazed at the tricks they played on one another.

"Níko, come out here," shouted Sotíris, relishing this moment when the veil was about to be drawn to reveal the mystery.

"What do you want?" asked Níkos, coming out panting and grimacing as if he had swallowed a hot pimento.

"Well now, son," said his father, sounding as if he pitied him, "are you suffering that much? Which leg's hurting you?"

"This one," said Níkos, and pointed to the bandaged one. But he looked a bit shaken at being put through such a fine sieve.

"Yes, but yesterday evening you bandaged the other one!"

Níkos looked his father straight in the eye. He seemed to remember, and in one leap disappeared like a bird.

Níkos didn't work for long in the furnace. He went into his brother's business. Antónis couldn't manage collecting both shares of the winnings all by himself. He made Níkos specialise in the cards and he specialised in the dice. "They're difficult customers here," said Antónis, proud that he was able to bridle them.

One of their crowd, Yánnis Thémas described Papaconstantínou's career: "At first he emerged as a pickpocket and a small-time thief. Then he made his mark as an expert at thimblerig and three card swindle. He's had a varied career, dealing in hashish and narcotics and involved in armed robberies with a fair number of stabbings."

He was in prison for years. There he acquired a mean, bloodthirsty look and he was feared by the other inmates.

Antónis was of medium height. When he walked he leaned to one side. He put on one sleeve of his jacket and the other sleeve hung down, hiding the two-edged knife in his red waistband. His eyes were red from his drug habit. When he looked at anyone he disliked, you would think he was shooting out sparks of fire at him. On his right cheek he had a deep scar. Yánnis Thémas said about that: "He got it from Bahtís." He was another gangster, the most notorious terrorist in Gazohóri. He ran the brothels in Voutádon Street.

"In a fierce fight Bahtís cut his cheek and Antónis stuck the knife in his knee. It left him crippled; since then he has to go about with a crutch . . . He's a bad lot, a violent man. In prison he even frightened the thieves. He rarely ever speaks.

He hides what he's thinking, not to let the others get above themselves and to make them fear and respect him. He has a hard look in his eye. His crimes are there, clear to see. Anyone who shows curiosity about his activities puts himself in danger. If Bahtís doesn't knife him he'll give him a slap on the face and chase him away, humiliated."

Thémas knew many stories like this. He was shortish and skinny. He spoke slowly and pretended to be a bit stupid, but his companions would tell you, he was a wily fox, a scum. They had nicknamed him Thémas[5] because every time he spoke he would make an exaggerated sign of the cross and say: "Lord help us. Lord forgive us, Great is thy mercy O Lord."

Thémas was well known as a most skilful burglar and a cool, determined thief. While he was emptying the shops and houses in Athens he didn't spare even the hovels.

One time he came up to the youngsters who were playing pitch-and-toss with five-leptá coins. "Come and I'll show you how to play Thirty-one,"[6] he said and sat on the ground. The children sat down with him. Soon he had taken all their money and started to leave. The children, very annoyed, looked at one another, and one of them said: "Give us the money, swindler."

"Lord forgive us, what are you saying? I have the right to it since I taught you the skill," said Yánnis in a frightened voice. Then he crossed himself as always and began to move

---

[5]Lord! or God! in Greek is Θεός (Theós). *Thémas* is an abbreviation of Θεέ μας (*Theé mas*) meaning "our Lord".

[6]Thirty-one is a card game like blackjack.

off again. The children grabbed stones, blocked his way and shouted threateningly, "The money, thief or you'll not escape." Thémas looked as if he had lost courage. He must have realised that he couldn't manage to get past these untameable little boys. He gave a false laugh, handed them back the money and said several times in order to escape: "I was only playing a joke on you. I wouldn't take your money," and he cleared off, but looking behind him all the time for fear a stone would accompany him. When the next time he was with his fellow gamblers one of them jeered at him: "Are you not ashamed? You tried to take the money from the children. You won't let them play alone to sharpen their wits?"

Their circle was made up of bullies. If Papaconstantínou didn't come to roll his own dice and deal his own cards the game didn't begin. Whoever else was thinking of rolling his own dice or dealing his own cards had to think twice.

Papaconstantínou wouldn't strike him with his hand; he hadn't great physical strength. He would strike him with the knife; he was amazingly nimble with it.

Out of those who dared to roll their own dice for a game, only one escaped stabbing. In front of the players Antónis took the offending dice and flung them away with a bullying gesture of bravado, and threw down his own for them to play with.

The others supported the one who was starting a revolt to get rid of Papaconstantínou. One of the supporters said: "We won't gain anything with the change. Somebody else'll get the upper hand. He could be worse than this one, my boys."

"Which one was it who took out his own dice?" Papaconstantínou asked, in a tone that showed he wasn't inclined to leave the rebel unpunished. Nobody spoke, but their eyes fell on the one who did it.

"Listen here you fool! Since it's you that played this trick on me I'll let you off this time, on account of your stupidity. I won't do you any harm for what you did. Get away from here and don't dare set foot in this place again!" and he gave him a kick on the behind with the pointed toe of the ankle boot that the tough guys were in the habit of wearing. The others, with heads bowed, showed their anger at his behaviour and at being separated from their friend.

Somebody, who was twice as big as Papaconstantínou, said to him in a hesitant tone: "Catch on slow, don't you pal."

Antónis seemed to have understood. The spirit of revolt was circulating around him, and he would have to put things right again. He glowered at him, put his finger on his lips and shouted hoarsely, "Shut up, I said!"

The bully would use the words "I said" at the end of his remarks, like an irrevocable command, lest his victim would dare to say another word, and get the knife instead of a reply.

One of the players had once said: "When Papaconstantínou isn't with us you'd think none of us thought much of him, but when we see him we tremble." Somebody else said: "To hold on to a reputation like his you need to be very tough and bloodthirsty, to sacrifice yourself at any moment, and have no regrets about slaughtering people."

They were seldom rounded up. The police hesitated to fight with them. Once I heard a policeman say: "We'd need a lot of men on the ground to go down there. We're dealing with gangsters, cold-blooded murderers. They aren't all like that. There are some really brave young men there."

A very tall man, straight as a cypress tree, called Yánnis Kapetanákis, commented: "The police aren't interested in coming for the stabbings that happen among themselves. They're interested in smuggled and stolen goods, in drugs that they deal in and smoke openly. These bums are destroying our children; they're converting them like repulsive preachers."

Kapetanákis looked favourably on them. He was a father; he had two sons.

The young people in the neighbourhood started smoking cigarettes early. They talked tough and were eager to acquire a surly attitude. The children savoured foul words as if they were sweets. They made their voice deep with a touch of hoarseness to imitate the language of the tough guys. They would compete with one another to be first to play cards, roll dice, and smoke hashish and cocaine, to be quarrelsome, to carry a knife and draw it on the slightest provocation. The adults, who served as prototypes, appeared satisfied to see the young people resembling them. They praised them for starting early on the road to dissipation.

"The boy will be a good dervish,"[7] they would say, and their eyes, red and heavy-looking with the drugs, would fill with admiration. As we listened to them we were fired with the desire to resemble our great teachers as quickly as possible. Our knowledge was considerably enriched in this school.

---

[7] dervish—*dervísi*—a brave young man (a Turkish word).

We would use words like "pal", "let's say", "stop it!", "hey tough guy", "I gotcha", and other such expressions.

Níkos Papaconstantínou, in front of everybody, would take the tobacco out of the bottom end of the cigarette and squeeze in a piece of hashish. He was very advanced for his age.

One day Níkos put the reefer in my mouth and said, as if he wanted to do me a favour: "Have a drag, brother!" I took a puff. It had a strong, unpleasant smell, like incense. I felt sick. They were all looking at me. I couldn't get out of it. It seemed to me that my manhood was being put to the test. In this neighbourhood if you didn't swim with the stream they would laugh at you and "give you a few slaps" as they said in their language.

During a sudden round-up by the police, with the help of the army, they caught Antónis Papaconstantínou. Níkos was ousted from the control of the card game. When, after a time, Antónis reappeared, somebody else was holding the position of dictator; he was Yórghos Kouloúkis, a sturdy man with coarse features and a stubborn and determined look in his eye.

One Sunday afternoon I saw a huge circle of people. In the middle of them were Antónis and Kouloúkis. Their jackets were wrapped round their left hand. In their right hand they held double-edged knives and they were fighting each other. When one leapt forward to strike, the other used his hand with the jacket wrapped round, as a shield. Antónis was more nimble, Kouloúkis stronger in driving him back. There were knife marks all over their bodies. Their clothes were sticking to them with blood and sweat. They were growling like wild beasts and every now and again they would bellow: "I'll drink your blood! I'll get you!"

The fight went on for hours. They looked exhausted. They stopped a few times. It was like a hostile truce. They sat at a distance from each other, breathing heavily, and then suddenly they would leap up shouting with rage: "I've got you. You're a dead man!" Near evening Antónis couldn't endure any longer, and fell. Kouloúkis knelt over him and stabbed him in the heart.

They carried them both away in a cart. Yórghos was hardly able to breathe with the pain of the knife wounds all over him. Next day they took away two dead bodies; Kouloúkis went soon after Antónis. He couldn't hold out against the wounds. The fight was heard of far and wide. The place where they fought became a historic site. For a time many people came down from all the neighbourhoods to see it. One of those who paid an unexpected visit said: "We've come to see the place, as if it were the one where Hector fought with Achilles."[8] Antónis's mother and father and sisters didn't weep for his death. One woman said: "Whatever tears his family had for him seem to have been used up when he took the wrong path."

The women of ill-repute who had settled down in Keratohóri didn't behave themselves even in the neighbourhood. They led young and old astray. They separated married

---

[8]"The place where Hector fought Achilles" was the plain of Troy where in Homer's "Iliad" the Trojan hero, Hector fought with the Greek hero, Achilles and Hector was slain.

couples. They broke up families. One of them, called Alexandra, made a particular impression. She had a very dark complexion, so they gave her the nickname Black. She was young and very beautiful. Someone called her a flower of the devil. When she came to our neighbourhood she brought with her a little daughter just about two years younger than me. She was very fair with big green eyes.

Black didn't go near anyone in the neighbourhood. Her dealings were with men outside. She would laugh at nothing and cry just as easily. There were times she would stay motionless for hours, her big black eyes wide open and running with tears. Nobody ever found out what she was seeing during those hours.

One time I heard her say to Ventoúraina: "I'm from a mountain village in Viotía. I was orphaned when I was a baby. I was brought up by one of my mother's sisters. When I was very young she gave me to a family as a servant. When I became a young girl the boss made me pregnant. To avoid a family scandal he gave me a little money and threw me out. The child looks so like that criminal. There are times I loathe her. I beat her and it feels like I'm beating him. I don't know what comes over me. I go mad. I beat her and then I regret it. I feel so miserable. I cry about the harm I'm doing to my child. But I beat her again and I hate her even more. And again I'm sorry and I cry about it. I don't know why I do it. My hatred for her gets stronger all the time."

With the beatings and the punishments the little girl grew weak. She became a skeleton; she became bed-ridden and her mother never looked after her. There was an elderly man Zervoudákis who had an old cart, drawn by a feeble little donkey. He would go and gather greens in the fields at Áyia Varvára. He had taken me on to help him. I would be given a piece of bread when I was there. I was away from the neighbourhood for two days. When I returned Little Baby, as they called the little girl, had died. We hadn't heard if she had a name. Some of the women said that her mother hadn't christened her.

Mihálaina, who was in the adjoining room, would repeat the story about the little girl: "In the last night she was burning with fever and got up to find the jug of water. She seemed to be searching carefully in the dark, for fear her mother would wake and beat her. Her mother heard her. She got up and gave her a thrashing. She was beating her and shouting wildly at her, as if she were crying: "*Still* you're here. Why don't you die and give me peace. I don't want to see you here in the morning, you cursed brat. You torment me."

In the morning they found her lying dead on the floor beside her bedding. Black had disappeared after dawn. The women in the neighbourhood wept for the little girl. Hrístaina, who let the room to Black, undertook to pay the funeral expenses. She was inconsolable. She had wanted to adopt the little girl and her mother wouldn't give her up. Every now and then Hrístaina would weep and shout out: "Aah, the scoundrel didn't give her to me. She preferred to give her to Háron."[9]

---

[9]In Modern Greek Χάρος (Háros) means Death. The name comes from the Ancient Greek mythology where Χάρων (Cháron) was the ferryman who rowed the dead across the rivers Styx and Acheron into the Underworld.

One girl, who was educated and who would write the letters in most of the houses of the neighbourhood said: "Black didn't give Little Baby to Hrístaina. If she lived she would see her and be tormented. And that was precisely what she wanted to avoid."

I was shaken by the death of the little girl. I suffered to see such a dreadful life seething before my eyes. My childish heart was filling with bitter experiences. But when I saw the sun, the moon, the stars, the mountains, the forests, and the plains a strong faith would flow through me—that something higher exists in this miracle called life.

Panayotis Tranoulis with the unforgettable Manos Katrakis and his wife Linda.

THE FURNACE

When Stámos left we were slow to begin work at our bench with a new moulder. A man as small as a child came to us from the island of Thermiá. He was called Kóstas and they changed his name to Kotsíkos, because of his small stature. Working in the furnaces was the hereditary occupation of the men from Thermiá. They came at the beginning of spring and left in the autumn when the rains began. From the beginning Kotsíkos didn't think I was capable of the work. Whenever I would go to take a mould he would look askance at me. When I didn't keep up with him he wouldn't speak. He wouldn't deign to. He'd look at me with indignation as if he were inwardly cursing me. When his pale blue eyes rested on me I felt a chill. He wasn't very nimble, and appeared to tire quickly. All day he panted and puffed to produce his quota of bricks.

The work that the moulders did was terribly tiring. It demanded all their strength. Their clothes would be sticking to them with sweat. Their aprons, made of sackcloth, would be soaking. The clay stuck to them and they would become very heavy. The moulders would complain that the aprons were cutting into them at the waist with the weight of the clay. When they stopped and threw them off they would make movements with their bodies from the pain, like

writing snakes, and say: "Aah, aah mother, my waist."
When you heard them say this it made you suffer with them
and clench your teeth in sympathy.

To make a brick the moulder threw a lump of the tempered clay into the mould. Then he sliced off the surplus clay
with a heavy stick—"the strike," as we called it. With the
water and the clay the "strike" became as heavy as iron. The
bottom of the mould was made of sheet iron, and when the
moulder wanted to hurt us he would throw the tempered clay
in before we could set it properly down and take the filled
one away, and our hands would be caught between the mould
and the bench. This could hurt like a door closing and
squeezing your fingers. It would have been better if he had
given us a hundred blows with a stick than have our hands
caught like this. Kotsíkos, who didn't want me to work with
him, trapped my hands every so often and they would burn
with the pain. Once, when he did this, he cut the tip off one
of my fingers, together with the nail. My mother healed my
cut finger with wax ointment. When it was partly healed and
I went back to work, Kotsíkos scolded me: "Tell me you little scoundrel, did you enjoy the rest? Was it good? Lazy ras-
cals. It's not your fault. It's the fault of those mothers of
yours, those jackdaws, who teach you to be like this."

My mother had told me that I should show the moulder
that my finger was not completely healed so that he would be
easier on me. But since he immediately spoke so harshly to
me I couldn't tell him, and held my tongue.

In the days when I was absent the "feeder" had been
replaced. A big stout man had come. His name was Bólmos,

a dangerous man and a stupid show-off. He had great physical strength, as have all who are somewhat stupid. He filled the wheelbarrow with clay almost to breaking point and brought it over to the bench ostentatiously, so that everyone would see him. One of those who knew how to rag people like this, called out: "My, my, Bólmos, look at you! You're the second Koutalianós!"[1] Bólmos raised his cap high as if he wanted them all to see him, opened his eyes wide, smiled and said loudly so that they would all hear him. "What can we do about the barrow! If it could take more clay I would bring a load that would keep the moulder working for an hour!" I was surprised that grown men would want to boast about such trivial things.

Bólmos did not get on well with Kotsíkos. He refused to acknowledge the moulder as his boss. He made it clear that he regarded him as a worthless little man. One day Bólmos said bluntly: "Slice the clay you've got on the bench and we'll have a break for a snack."

"Won't you bring some more loads and we'll eat with the other benches?" said the moulder in a timid voice, full of hesitation.

"You're not right in the head," retorted Bólmos. "You're always saying silly things. If the others go to the sea and drown themselves, are we going to go as well?" and he looked sideways at the moulder as if to say: "I don't take orders."

---

[1]Panayótis Koutalianós was a professional wrestler. He became famous between 1882–1892, not only for his prowess but also because he wore a tiger skin when wrestling. He came from the island of Koutáli.

Kotsíkos gave him a covert, sidelong glance. He looked as if he was seething with anger but wasn't going to quarrel with this foolish Heracles.[2] Bólmos didn't fear dismissal. The union regarded him and some others like him as its bravest young men. If the workers had a dispute with the bosses the president of the union took these men with him and settled it. They were determined terrorists, much feared. They weren't afraid of the police. Some of them wouldn't give way if they were threatened with a pistol to their head. The gendarmerie that policed the countryside was conciliatory and powerless. During general strikes it got help from the army. A Roumanian wrestler had heard about Bólmos. He called in at the furnace and suggested that they should have a match, but Bólmos refused. The older men, who knew that Bólmos wouldn't quarrel with them, when they saw him passing, would say to one another just to annoy him: "What strong arms that Roumanian has. His neck and head are all of a piece!"

The Roumanian even gave a display. He drove several size seventy nails into a piece of wood. He twisted them a number of times right and left with one hand and broke them off like leeks. He proposed that Bólmos should break one. Again he refused, and they took the opportunity to torment him with sly digs.

---

[2]Heracles, known as the great Hercules by the Romans, was a legendary figure of Greek mythology, son of Zeus and Alcméne. He was famous for his great physical strength and for having accomplished twelve gigantic tasks imposed upon him.

Kopsós, who was a tease and was much respected, whenever he saw Bólmos, would approach him and say: "What a devil of a man that Roumanian is to be able to cut off size seventy nails with his teeth!"

Bólmos would laugh when he heard this. He pretended to be amused. But his big ears would go red and he looked annoyed. Sometimes he would say as well: "Not with the *teeth*, man!"

Kotsíkos himself, who attempted a harmless joke, had the devil to pay. Bólmos looked at him out of the corner of his eye with contempt and retorted: "Knock it off you blockhead—trying to be clever. Old sour milk and whey!"

The people on the island of Thermiá had barren mountains for fields. They kept some goats and sheep and a feeble cow and with these they were careful to eke out their food for the year. They made cheese with the milk they produced and this was why they were generally called wheyeaters. When anyone called them by this nickname they took great offence. One time the moulder, Pisadákis, annoyed with Bólmos said: "He humiliates Kotsíkos who's under his thumb. But if he had the Roumanian as the moulder would he behave badly to *him*? We can all put on airs before the weak. We don't realise that we become worth spitting at."

An old man called Mikés from one of the islands had the last word: "A man shouldn't act clever too much and put on airs because somebody'll come along and make him shut up."

Bólmos, who had the moulder under his thumb, would retort every so often: "Shut up, whey-face! What do *you* know whey-face? Who takes any notice of *you*, whey-face?"

Bólmos was younger than Kotsíkos and I was upset to hear him behaving so badly towards him. The moulder would talk to us about his poverty. He was in great need. He had a wife and children, and I was sorry to see that from the efforts of those weak hands they were expecting him to bring them bread. I was generally moved by this person who was a man in years but in stature looked like a child. It moved me to see him struggle to get through his day, like me. Even the moustache under his nose looked false to me. I pitied him for that too.

Kotsíkos had got into a row with this coarse man. One time when he tried to assert his rights Bólmos opened his eyes wide, raised his fist in the air and showed his dog's teeth; you would have thought he was going to tear Kotsíkos in pieces, and he yelled at him: "Watch out. Don't say another word or I'll give you one that'll knock you two metres into the ground!"

The moulder was humiliated. He was shaking all over as he worked nervously. He scolded me for not being on time with the mould. Twice I saved my hands that he was about to trap with the mould. The first attempt nearly took one of my fingers off and made me jump with the pain. "Run you little scoundrel!" he shouted at me each time I was behind, and became more and more angry with me. I wasn't the only one who wasn't keeping up with him. The other two boys, older and more capable than me, weren't keeping up either.

It was a long time yet until the end of the shift and he was urging us on prematurely. At one moment, at the height of my tiredness and dizziness, I don't understand what possessed him; he raised the "strike" and gave me a blow on the left shoulder. With the shock I fell in a heap, taking the mould with me. Kotsíkos yelled at me: "Get up, you, get up!" He must have thought I could get up and I was not. He came over where I had fallen and gave me a hard kick in the ribs to force me to get up. The two other carriers pulled me to the side, to continue with the work until I recovered. Kopsós, who was further away, saw what happened. He came up and said to the boys: "Give him some water to drink, will you? He's parched. Don't you see he's blue in the face?"

And he turned to the moulder and said: "Shame on you Kotsíkos, I wouldn't have expected it of you. Why didn't you give him another blow to finish him off on the spot and not have him writhing in pain like this? And you a family man. Don't forget you have children too." Kopsós went off and I dragged myself after him. Someone said to Kopsós: "You were right to give him a piece of your mind. If he has any feeling he'll understand what you said."

"It looks like he's understood already," someone else butted in. "Don't you see? He's bowed his head like Judas the moment he decided to hang himself." I turned round and saw him. He looked miserable, as if he were bitterly sorry. I pitied him and wept for him and for me and for every vulnerable person in the world.

In the furnace there wasn't a carrier to replace me and they put my brother Alékos in my place. He was two years older than me and taller, but he wasn't very strong. He had less strength than I had. At first they put him at the bench as a carrier. He couldn't endure it and came off that job. Then they put him to work stacking the bricks in rows one on top of the other with spaces between; it was a way of drying them. His daily wage for this work was very little.

The grownups would look at me and say: "This child is a marvel! So young and able to endure this heavy work!"

I endured it, but how I endured it nobody could know; only I knew it in my heart. "The grocer's and baker's account books are full. If we don't pay they will stop our credit and I'll die of hunger," I wanted to say, but didn't.

When I managed to get back home I found my mother ill in bed. There was a bowl of water and vinegar beside her. She was wetting pieces of cloth in it and putting them to her temples to alleviate her headache and get rid of the fever.

As soon as she saw me coming in leaning to the side and groaning she forgot about herself, jumped up and began to weep and shout: "Dear Jesus, Holy Mother, they've killed my child! Don't they fear God? Haven't *they* got children? Do they not know about poverty and orphans?"

She turned to a corner of the wall where there were two or three black, wooden, worm-eaten icons, and throwing her arms wide she said: "Dear God, wouldn't it have been better to take *me*? But you went and took their father who could bring them a mouthful of bread?"

Weeping and lamenting like this she washed me and wiped the clay off me that the "strike" had covered me with. Hearing her cries and shouts some women neighbours gathered.

"Look, the criminal has killed him. His shoulder's black, the poor child," said Stéfaina who was a good woman. Her husband had a little taverna in the neighbourhood.

She hastened to give my mother some consolation: "The day before yesterday didn't he send mine back all bleeding, that savage Aléxis Skamángas?"

A tall, thin old woman who wore glasses and was called Zaharákaina wrinkled her nose and screwed up her eyes to see me better. Scarcely touching me with one finger on my shoulder she said: "But his shoulder's infected. Go to the police." Her husband was formerly a gendarme. He had been dismissed from the force but they continued to go to the police to resolve all their disputes.

Mrs Hrístaina, our neighbour, who always stood by us, brought a bowl of boiled oil and camomile and dabbed it over my wounded shoulder. All the women spoke highly of her and respected her as the most well off woman in the neighbourhood since she owned her own little house. She had a goat and hens and her husband, who worked as a tanner, had a regular wage. When the skins were brought to the tanners, they had little pieces of meat sticking to them. "Her husband gathers the pieces and they make meatballs and have cooked meals," said Mrs Antónaina.

It was a while before I went back to work and when I went I wasn't capable of carrying the moulds. The pain in my shoulder became permanent. They put me to work "outside" which meant that there were no fixed hours. We worked from dawn to dark. Heading the "outside" workers was Apostólis. He was an old man, older than all of them, tall, thin and white-haired. From bending so much over his work he had a hump and they called him Apostólis, the hunchback. He was polite and spoke with a smile. When he had to show something about the work to someone inexperienced and even to us young ones, he never said: "Do it like this." He would say instead: "If you want you can do it like this," and he would show us how the work should be done.

At lunchtime when the workers gathered and spread their napkins to have a bite to eat, you would always hear something good from Apostólis. Once I was just in time to hear him say: "I haven't got the right to try to be clever, to advise. I can give my opinion only when I'm asked."

At lunchtime I couldn't be near them to hear what they said. For lunch I always had just plain bread and sometimes I had nothing and I was ashamed to sit with the others. When I hadn't anything to eat and was sitting near them they noticed and would always give me something. I was moved by their gesture but I couldn't swallow it because I could see that I was taking it off them.

At break-times when I hadn't anything to eat I would sit farther away and when I saw that they had finished eating I would come up to the group pretending that I had eaten too. When we started work again Apostólis would come discreetly over to me and say: "Tell me, have you eaten?" I would remember his kindness at other times when I was alone and it brought tears to my eyes. I would always say to myself: "How wonderful it is to be good." Many times Apostólis would offer me some food from his napkin. I was hungry but I wouldn't take it. One morning when we met on the road he greeted me as if we were of the same age. "Good-day Panayótis, how are you?" he said cheerfully and gave me his hand to shake. Then immediately his tone changed.

"Aah, aah, we old ones go to work before the light of day and you, a little child, follow us. You should be resting at this hour."

I wasn't able to reply, and stayed silent, but inwardly I had a thousand good thoughts about him. After a while he spoke again: "You're a polite and willing boy. You're not like the others who are disobedient. You speak to them and they mock you and talk in obscenities."

I knew the obscenities only I didn't utter them, and have never been in the habit of using them throughout my life; they don't appeal to me at all.

Apostólis was always telling me that I had good traits in my character, and I tried, if I hadn't got them, to acquire them. Every time I heard this marvellous man, I would borrow from his goodness. I wanted to resemble him.

The work outside that they gave me to do was to give water to the workers to drink and to go around with a wheelbarrow and gather up the broken bricks. I would put a few in the barrow and these I would place on the right hand side; the other side I left empty.

I wasn't able to lift weights. The shoulder I was beaten on tired quickly and became rigid with pain.

Apart from Apostólis, Nikólas Retetángos, a stout man, was also a foreman. One time he saw me piling the broken bricks into the barrow on the one side and shouted at me: "What are you doing there skinny boy? Are you playing?"

He spoke so roughly to me I don't know how I was able to make him understand. As soon as he heard he looked me all over. "So that's why you're putting them in like that. The shoulder still hurts you?" he said in a softened tone and went off looking sorry for me.

The next day at lunchtime when they were all together eating, as I was passing, Nikólas called me: "Come here, my friend." He also made a signal to me with his hand to approach. I went over. "Sit down," he said and moved up to make room for me next to him on some bricks. I sat down. He was behaving so kindly to me I was expecting something good. Beside me sat Níkos, a fine upstanding young man who was always singing. Apostólis had said about him: "May he always be well. He gives us pleasure. He sings like a goldfinch."

So he was stuck with the nickname Goldfinch. Nikólas shook out his napkin and gathered up the tins. It looked as if he was thinking and had forgotten me. At one point, as if freeing himself of something that was troubling him, he said: "It's not right when one strives to improve what one has to say. People should tell the truth and only the truth; nothing is more beautiful than that. To speak as you feel, as your heart itself tells you."

Níkos the Goldfinch, smiling asked him: "What's the matter, master?" They called the foreman "master" out of respect and because he was very good at the work.

"It's something that's been bothering me," said Nikólas and stopped.

"Are *we* not to know about it? Is it a secret?" asked Goldfinch again.

"It's not a secret. It's that I do things in a hurry without thinking, and I make stupid mistakes. I see one of you doing a job and at first glance it doesn't look right to me. I scold him and when he explains to me why he's doing it like that I realise that he's right. The work had to be done the way he's done it. I'm immediately stricken with remorse. I say to myself that I shouldn't be hasty but I get caught out again. Then when we're sitting together my bad behaviour comes to mind. I see you and I'm ashamed. Yesterday I made a mistake again. I scolded the orphan who comes to work crippled, to earn his bread, and all night I suffered, I felt such guilt. I ask forgiveness from you all, even from the child."

Here his voice broke. He didn't speak for some time.

When he recovered he spoke again: "It's as if this confession to you has lifted a great weight from me. I feel something new, as if I've taken communion without realising. I remember the words of some very fine people I worked with when I was young. What would I give to be able to find them again and say a big thank you to those people, most of whom are no longer alive." He bowed his head. You would have thought he was going to burst into tears and would never stop. Next day at lunchtime a soft voice was heard asking: "So those moulders you were telling us about yesterday didn't beat you, Nikólas?" It was a thin young man who rarely spoke, but his remarks were as grave as an old man's. "They beat us Pandelákis for our own good," murmured Nikólas and after a moment continued: "Always forget the bad things and remember the good things Pandelákis. And when somebody gives you a job to do and he benefits from it, don't look at what he has gained from you; look at how you have benefited from him."

"Congratulations, Nikólas, on the important words you've just said! You've moved me very much," said Kopsós, and he grasped his hand. "It takes courage to tell the truth. When you tell it you're free, and to be envied. You have earned love."

He thought for a moment and went on in a more quiet tone: "Now that you have set the example, how beautiful the truth is! You show us how to talk about our weaknesses with pride and not to avoid the truth as we think up the lie and give it priority."

All these things I heard there became a magical song within me. I had never heard a more beautiful one and I think I'll never stop hearing it. From that day Nikólas won my heart. Whenever I saw him standing I would go to him as if he were my father or my big brother. Once, when Nikólas was sitting with a group I went and sat beside him. Without realising, I put my hand in his pocket. I stayed like that with my mind elsewhere. When we rose to go back to work Nikólas felt my hand in his pocket and smiling, said to me: "Hey you, you put your hand in my pocket." Others saw it and didn't think anything of it. I felt ashamed and I still torment myself about it.

In autumn, when the rains intensified, work stopped at the benches. Kotsíkos put his clothes in a sack, said goodbye to everyone and went on his way. Nikólas Retetángos, as he watched him walking away, said, his voice breaking: "In autumn one by one we take the road of farewell. The clouds are low and the air smells of rain. Yet another winter comes and brings with it unemployment and uncertainty." When

Nikólas stopped speaking he waved his hand as if saying goodbye to the moulder Kotsíkos who was disappearing in the distance. It was over, like a stifling emotional interlude.

Goldfinch said to me: "Tell me, did Kotsíkos say goodbye to you?" And he gave me a searching look, which suggested that it should have happened. *I* hadn't given it a thought. But when Goldfinch mentioned it I was sorry it hadn't happened. Mariólis Drakoúlis, an exceptionally fine young man, who distinguished himself on account of his good character, said with a sad serious tone: "It doesn't matter. He doesn't need a farewell, since Kotsíkos left him such a big souvenir."

I understood that it was about my shoulder and as my heart was heavy with the departure of the moulder whom I might not see again, I couldn't control myself; I began sobbing in front of them. They listened to me silently for a moment and then Drakoúlis rebuked me: "Stop it, you fool. Is it proper for men to cry?" but he gave Goldfinch a meaningful look, as if he excused my behaviour. Years had passed before I met Kotsíkos again. My heart leapt. Time beautifies the past. I thought I was seeing a close relative whom I so much wanted to see again. He was old now and his hair was completely white. It seemed to me unfortunate that someone would be old and very small. I thought to myself: "An old man ought to be taller than a young man, so that he can command respect with his height as well as with his experience of life."

Kotsíkos asked me about work and if I was married, if I had children and how many, if they were boys or girls. He asked me about many things. He didn't talk to me about our work in the past. I in my turn asked him about his children;

I asked about them by name, one by one. This impressed him and he said: "Heavens, what a memory you have!" I was surprised that he told me I had a memory. How could it be otherwise? That I should forget? That's life. Should I forget my own life? Then why do we live? But then I didn't know if this was because of my good memory or because of the stories he told us at work about his poverty and his children and I had felt somehow related to him. At one moment he asked me if I remembered him. Even if I had wanted to I wouldn't have been able to forget him. The pain from the blow he gave me as a child with the "strike" on the shoulder had crippled me and will leave me only when I close my eyes for ever. When I was young I felt the pain in my shoulder whenever I got very tired or sat where there was no support for my back. I always took care of the arm on this side and put the weight on the other side. Now, at the age I've reached, the pain in my shoulder is permanent and is often unbearable. Sometimes it stabs like a knife in me and I can't breathe. I cry with the terrible pain. I've fought it with ointments, medicines, massage, medicinal baths, steam baths, and other things. Why should I tell him all this? Did I want to break his heart? At one time we had a relationship in poverty. Now, at the age that we've reached, we have a closer relationship. We are related by the inevitable, by death.

The water that we drank we took from the well that also supplied the water for the bricks. From August to September there was very little water in the well. It became muddy and when I was giving it to the workers to drink, they would look daggers at me, swear at me and threaten me: "What kind of water's this you're bringing us to drink, you little rascal! Are you throwing mud into it? I'll pull your ears off!" Sometimes they would give me a slap.

Apostólis intervened on one occasion: "Hey, hold on a minute, moulders. Why are you getting at the child? You've picked on this child to curse and threaten *him*, even to beat him—the least responsible for this business? Don't you see the water running muddy out of the pipe? Where can he find any better water to bring us?"

There was also a rough-mannered, slightly crazy fellow that they made fun of. When he first came to work they gave him the nickname Loverboy because when he talked about girls he called them lovers. He was very good-looking and talked obscenely about his relationships with women, vilifying them and degrading them mercilessly. The others were obscene too when they talked about women, but he was in the vanguard.

One time Loverboy took the tin of water I gave him to drink and threw it in my face. "You make us sick, you little bastard, giving us this water to drink!" he said, looking satisfied with himself. The water soaked me all down my front and trickled down inside my clothes to my feet. Apostólis touched his beard and said: "Shame on you, Loverboy, a grown man like you treating the orphan like this. Look at the state he's in!" The word "orphan" struck me to the heart and I began to cry. I had heard them calling me "orphan" before. I paid no attention to it. But this time I felt it differently. This time it hurt. I saw myself as an insignificant little thing, thrown carelessly by fate into the boundless ocean of life.

"I only did it for a joke, man," Loverboy replied indifferently. When the boss came, although the clothes were sticking to me and I was shivering with cold, I began to work. The boss noticed me and said: "How did you get into that state, tell me." I didn't reply, but went on working and crying at the same time. "Loverboy soaked him," somebody said. "The child gave him water to drink and he threw it in his face."

The boss heard this with indifference and turned to leave. "He said he threw it in his face because it was muddy," the worker called out quickly behind the boss before he could walk away. He stressed the word "muddy" to make the boss pay attention to it. The boss appeared not to notice, but fired Loverboy, and pretended that he fired him for my sake. In the evening I went home sick. I had fits of shivering and was feverish. I had caught a severe chill and was in bed for days. When I went back to work one morning into the shed, it was still dark.

"Little Panayótis, say hello to us!" cried old Apostólis who was sitting on some bricks. In the dark I couldn't see him immediately. I was taken by surprise. There wasn't only Apostólis, there was Goldfinch and Kóstas Vláhos, a tall dark man who knew how to speak correctly and had a deep bass voice. I liked to listen to him. "What was wrong with you? We heard you were ill," said Vláhos, shaking his fine head. I was pleased he asked me the question. He had taken no notice of me before.

"What do you expect?" Kóstas continued. "Going out at his age to earn a day's wage at this barbarous work, it's well he's still alive. With people like Kotsíkos around . . ." I couldn't help being confused by these people. At work they became ill-tempered, they swore, they were unjust, and they rarely laughed or told a joke. They misunderstood every remark, and they were quick to take offence. They blasphemed and complained insufferably all the time. Each wanted to appear tough before the other, so that everyone would be afraid of him. They quarrelled and beat each other for no serious reason. They turned into disgusting brawlers. Enmity and jealousy simmered among them. One time I said to Apostólis: "Why is that?" Shaking his head he said: "Tiredness reduces them to that. It befuddles their brain. It breaks their nerves. It invades them like opium. It doesn't let them think straight or distinguish between one person and another. When the tiredness leaves them, they're different people entirely. They become good men. They're ashamed of their faults. They can't believe the things they've done; they even deny their own words, because the words are not really theirs."

Apostólis was right. When they weren't working and I heard them talking I could see that they were sensible people; they had feelings and were compassionate. I was overwhelmed by those feelings. I wanted to hug them all, to hold them tight, to merge in with them and become one with them.

"You'll have no more trouble about the water now. The boss has put in a tank and he's bringing the water from outside," Apostólis told me.

"Poor Loverboy paid the price for us to drink clean water," said Goldfinch.

"It's always the way. Someone has to pay first so that the

others benefit," murmured Vláhos. And after a moment he went on: "The boss didn't dismiss Loverboy because he cares about his little worker. If he cared about his workers he wouldn't give us such water to drink. He fired Loverboy because he was the reason that he was compelled to bring clean water in from outside and spend money on it. Bosses care about their money; they don't care about us. And Loverboy didn't soak the child as he said, for a joke. He felt under pressure and in his tiredness his mind became confused and he didn't think who was in front of him. He threw the water on the child as if he was the culprit." He paused for a while and then he said: "And the things Loverboy said about girls he didn't say them to find fault with them. He said them out of compassion for us. He saw that we got tired and wanted to make us laugh, to console us. The boss fired him and now you see we have the feeling that something is missing from among us."

Apostólis sighed: "Aah, aah," and got up.

The other workers further along, were beginning to work.

The boss knew I had been ill. So that he wouldn't lose his authority over us, when he saw me working, he said in a tone of annoyance: "What happened to *you* again, tell me? Sometimes you'll go and sometimes you'll come? You've found your refuge in here?"

He didn't tell me to leave, and walked on.

One of the workers commented: "He profits from these children. He gives them very little in return for the work they do for him. And he's always saying he keeps them out of charity."

That worker was always making up jokes. Once he was holding a bank note and looking at it for a long time. "I'm losing patience seeing you do that. What are you looking for in that note?" Kóstas Vláhos asked him.

He smiled, as if he had done it on purpose to provoke Kóstas, and replied: "They say that these hung Christ on the cross, and I was looking to see what side they've hung him on."

"How did you do? Did you see him?"

"I didn't see him."

"How about yourself whom they hang on the cross from morning to night, for these notes? Did you happen to see *him* anywhere there?" Vláhos asked and gave him a shove.

LEAKOS

Among the workers was an undesirable type called Mít-sos Leákos who played the role of spy. Whatever happened at work he would run to tell the boss about it. He first started on this path by bringing love-letters to Krápas's mistresses. In time he made further progress. He became his spy among the work force. And they used to talk about something else to his detriment. He had two sisters of loose morals, as the adults would say. And the boss would have his way with them.

Behind his back the workers ran Leákos down. One time Pisadákis commented on him: "His horns are as high as the telegraph poles and the pimp doesn't take his sisters in off the streets instead of going and betraying one or the other of *us*."

Someone else said: "Does anyone who has a good reputation do these things? Only somebody who comes from a home where there are no morals does them."

Leákos didn't listen to what they said at his expense. He knew very well what they said and he was indifferent to it. All day he would laugh and sing and tell jokes. He appeared to be the happiest of men with a clear conscience, doing his work well. He was the only one who could go from one job to the other. He would leave the work inside the furnace and go to work outside. From there he would go to the perforator.[1] When he went to where old Apostólis was in charge, as soon as he saw him Apostólis would say to his workers: "Men, Leákos is coming. Watch what you say."

Nikólas said the same to the men he was supervising. The boss had a younger brother who worked for a daily wage. Whenever he saw Leákos, even he would shrink with fear.

Leákos didn't give orders. He wasn't a supervisor. He would only pass by and observe. When the workers saw him coming towards them they would start saying among themselves: "The pimp, the prize bastard!"

"Hi!." Leákos would greet them as if he were greeting his most cordial friends. They would return his greeting in the same good spirits. It was difficult for me to understand how they could adjust and play this insipid comedy.

One time, as Goldfinch was working, he dropped a pile of unfired perforated bricks and there was a fair amount of damage. Old Apostólis sent some workers to help him cover up the damage so that the boss wouldn't know about it. They gathered up the undamaged bricks, threw away the broken ones, and cleared away the fragments so that nothing was seen. At the last moment Leákos saw them. Goldfinch went pale and said bitterly: "The sneak! What the devil is he doing here?"

The next day the boss interrogated Goldfinch: "What happened yesterday?" He didn't reply. He stood looking at him, frightened. "Hey, didn't you hear me? I'm asking what

---

[1] perforator—*koufiomihaní*—was the first hand-made machine in Greece to produce perforated bricks.

happened yesterday?" he said again and shook him by the shoulders. Goldfinch remained silent. The boss became furious. He raised his fist and punched him twice in the face. Níkos began to bleed. His hair was tousled. I was upset to see him hurt and bleeding and my eyes filled with tears. Bosses hit their workers hard for the slightest thing.

Níkos was a handsome young man. He had a heart of gold and he sang very beautifully. When you heard him sing, you could forgive him much on account of his God-given gift.

Leákos swanned around the furnace as if nothing had happened. He laughed, sang, and told jokes as if he had achieved something very important. The workers seethed inwardly. They didn't speak out in front of him. They were on guard even behind his back. Among the work force there was even someone who begged Leákos to intervene with the boss to give him better work with a higher wage.

Once Pisadákis said about Leákos: "We see that even the most worthless can find followers. That's why good in the world is slow to come."

I avoided going near Nikólas from the day that, without realising it, I had put my hand in his pocket. He would call out to me now and again: "My friend, come here."

When I went to him he would always say something good to me and would ask: "Does your shoulder hurt?"

I was grateful to him that he worried about me.

On the morning that the boss hit Goldfinch, as I was passing by with the wheelbarrow, Nikólas called to me: "My friend, come here, we would like to see you." I went and stood in front of him and waited for what he would say:

"First of all say good-day to us and then we'll talk," said Nikólas, smiling. "Good-day," I said loudly.

"Good, now we can talk. But you, who are so polite, why don't you say good-day?" he asked, still smiling.

What was this "*you* are polite," again that he came out with. I felt numbness in my jaws and was unable to reply. Curious that he and Apostólis would say this to me now and again: "You're polite, willing, and hard-working. You don't tell lies. You don't use bad language . . . " All this made me watch what I did and what I said. Moreover, because of their remarks which showed the respect they had for my father, I had to maintain a certain seriousness.

"What did you think about the boss hitting Goldfinch?" Nikólas asked me, giving me a lively look with his big, alert eyes. "The boss is not to blame. Mítsos Leákos is to blame," I said. Nikólas started laughing louder. When he calmed down he said: "Good, who told you this?"

"No one, I see it myself," I replied.

"Bravo, congratulations, you are very observant," he said half joking, half serious. He shook my hand and continued: "Only one thing. Not that the boss was not to blame. The boss is most to blame for taking the time to listen to that pimp."

"Behind his back you all curse Leákos and to his face you talk as if he was your best friend," I said, expressing my great perplexity.

Nikólas laughed loudly. When he stopped he said to me: "You observed very well. One can speak to you as one could to an adult, but I'll teach you one thing: the hand that you can't bite, you should kiss. It isn't only Christ who has power; the Devil has power too. One does good and the other evil. We can't but take into account the power of evil." He glanced round as if he were expecting to see something, and said: "We don't want the Evil One. He's hateful to us; the power of his wickedness makes us speak to him."

THE STRIKE

There was something in the wind at the furnace. The men seemed restless. They were talking secretly to one another. One morning we went to work and there were no adults at the furnace. Kopsós was tending the fire all by himself. From among the children none of us was absent. We went to him.

"Did they not tell *you* not to come?" Kopsós asked us surprised.

"No," replied Liólios.

When Liólios spoke he took on a serious tone and I liked him. I always sought to imitate him. He was quite a plethoric boy, which was rare at the time and at his age.

"Go back to your homes. There's a strike on today. Look, *I'm* finishing the firing soon. I'll do the last batch and then I'm going. It wouldn't have been right to go off and leave it. There would have been great damage done. I sent my two helpers away yesterday evening. For my sake they would have stayed. I didn't want to make them into strike-breakers, so I stayed here alone. I have a duty to do this. The boss is my cousin. I'm justified."

Kopsós impressed me. An adult man, with authority, was sitting giving an explanation to us children. He showed respect for young people. He wanted to be a good example to them. I was pleased that we had found an adult who took us children into consideration. The other adults didn't care about us. One time I heard him say: "Children are the living flowers of life." When we were moving off Kopsós called to us: "Come here."

When we came to him he said to us: "Today in Botanicós the Workers' Solidarity is giving out bread and herrings to all the workers. You go along too and get some."

As soon as we arrived home Leákos came and gathered us. "Come to work, the boss says."

When we went back to the furnace we found a strange moulder there. One or two of the older boys knew him. "Níkos the Cockroach," said one of them, and explained. "His surname is Katsarós. Since he's skinny they changed his name to Katsarídas, the Cockroach."

Although it wasn't his job, the moulder Katsarídas helped in all the preparation of the moulding bench with great willingness.

"Look at how he's doing it!" said Liólios about Cockroach. "Like somebody starting his own business with the dream of succeeding."

Liólios said many things like this. We would take them as jokes and burst out laughing. He had some education; he had got through three classes in the primary school. To us illiterates he seemed like a professor. Pandelís, the boss, had as a partner, his elder brother Stávros. He was in charge of the business outside the factory. He would come to the furnace for two or three hours and only to the office.

He was fat and had to use a walking-stick. He wore collared shirts, trousers with a crease, and every so often a new hat. He hadn't a good reputation. They talked about him being a police spy. He was the enemy of the workers who used to say he had done battles against them. A drunk and a womanizer, he beat his wife in front of his children and now and again they came close to separating. Someone at the furnace had said about him: "His wife is a little old, a bit plain-looking, a very good housekeeper and from a good home. He married her for her money and they built the furnace. He doesn't look like much either; he has the face of a bum. He had a licence to carry arms and would let the pistol be seen in his back pocket."

He was boasting that he got the work going at the bench in order to break the strike. That day he didn't leave the furnace. He had provided his brother and some cousins with pistols. He was going around with the pistol in his hand saying in a loud voice: "Whoever dares to set foot in here will die on the spot."

Liólios, smiling ironically, said quietly: "He's shouting out of fear, to give himself courage because he knows he's getting scared."

When anyone passed by in the distance they would watch every movement in the smallest detail.

"Look at that one in black going past glancing cautiously over here. The strikers must have sent him," said big boss, Stávros.

"He's not wearing black. It's grey he's wearing," replied a tall man in their group.

"He's wearing black," Pandelís, the younger boss confirmed.

Liólios smiled and commented: "They're mixing up the colors out of fear; everything looks black to them. And when the younger boss insists that the passerby wore black, he's not sure. He insists on it in order to maintain his brother's authority, which also shows that he admires him."

About the moulder Cockroach, Liólios said ironically: "He's looking about him so many times for the strikers out of fear, more than he would have looked about him, waiting for his wife to pass by, when he was in love with her."

Someone came whom the bosses had sent to see where the strikers were and if there were many of them. "There was a big crowd of them. They were very wild. They were saying they'd bring down the scabs and the bosses with them."

"You didn't hear what way they'll be coming?" asked the frightened boss Pandelís.

"No, I only heard they'll divide into groups to raise a hue and a cry."

"Tell me, was Karamítsos with them?" Pandelís asked again.

"Yes, he was," the other replied dispiritedly, looking him in the eye and showing regret that he was bringing them such a piece of bad news. Karamítsos, who was the finest man in the union, was president. He was a giant, two heads above everyone else. He was sturdily built, each arm the size of a well-fed child, and his fingers were the size of our arms. He had a big moustache like a twisted meat hook and he always carried a big stick. He was famed for his boldness and bravery. Once I heard someone say about him: "When he's on your side you feel safe and proud. And when he's your opponent you're frightened at the thought of having to fight him. When he launches into a brawl, he becomes a whirlwind carrying whatever is in front of him." It was said that the first time Karamítsos became president and went to the ministry with two or three men from the committee to make a request on behalf of the union, the minister was taken aback when he saw such a giant. He immediately rose to his feet and welcomed him. When they sat down the men from the union made their requests to the minister and he replied: "This doesn't happen for anyone. I'll do it only for this man here," and he pointed to Karamítsos.

A close second to Karamítsos, Manólis Kokkinoyénis, who was very belligerent, was also coming. The bosses and their group remained thoughtful and motionless with their eyes wide open as if they were seeing something that was terrifying them.

At midday they didn't let us go home to eat. The bosses fed us. They were afraid the strikers might find us and prevent us from coming back to work.

More than ten or a dozen of us children and three adults were strike-breakers. Liólios was a carrier, like us. Because of this great shortage of workers they initiated him as a "feeder". Another strike-breaker said about him: "He's beefy. He can stand anything. He looks as if he's crazy about the new job, perhaps secretly thinking that after the strike, fate will raise him up a few steps."

They praised Liólios for his cleverness. Someone said:

"He's a marvel; has a terrific brain. He should have studied and become a lawyer, a diplomat or something like that."

In the afternoon two gendarmes and a sergeant came; there were altogether ten pistols guarding us. The news they brought was bad. A crowd of strikers was heading towards us.

As soon as Leákos and the other strike-breakers heard this, they disappeared. "Boss, shall I stop work?" Cockroach the moulder, terrified, asked Pandelís.

Stávros shouted an obscenity and turning his pistol on him he said: "Don't move from your place!"

Liólios said about the big boss: "He's not letting him go. If work stopped at the bench he'd look ridiculous to the other bosses. And he wants to play the hero." The sergeant, who wore a heavy moustache and behaved like a peasant, stated: "I haven't been ordered to shoot at them. We can only shoot to intimidate them."

"Shall I stop, boss until they've gone and then we can continue?" Cockroach asked again in a more despairing tone.

"I said don't leave your bench, or *you'll* be the first to die," said the big boss forcing him to stay at his place again. I could see that the moulder, Cockroach was a wretched man, a slave. I pitied him. About us children nobody cared. We were slaves of slaves.

"There! They're in sight," said a gendarme, terrified. We all looked where he was pointing. "When I first saw the gendarmes coming," said Liólios, "I thought we had great strength on our side. But now I see them looking around terrified to find a way to get out quickly."

I can still see that terrible black mass coming right for us, like a gigantic dragon, to swallow us all in one gulp. As the multi-legged beast approached, the bosses and their group were shooting in desperation to drive it away. It was hurrying fearlessly towards us. At its head we could see Karamítsos with Manólis Kokkinoyénis.

As soon as the crowd approached, Karamítsos shouted fiercely: "Shoot, you cowards!" and dashed inside.

Manólis Kokkinoyénis next to him, let out a hair-raising yell "Stand, Krápa, you son of a bitch and we'll have it out!"

Men rushed in with them like a whirlwind upon us with clubs, metal bars, and stones. The bosses, with the others, took to their heels. The strikers followed them close behind. Cockroach fell into their hands. One of the strikers shouted fiercely at me: "To hell, with you too!" He lifted the back of his hand to me, but it didn't come down on me. A carrier, who was working with me, said in a terrified voice: "Take off the apron, you runt and not show you're working. You'll have us all in danger," and he pulled the apron off me.

The invaders were smashing whatever they found— benches, wheelbarrows, moulds, tools, bricks, and the perforator. They left nothing undamaged.

When the strikers went away a crowd of people from the neighbourhood gathered and our mothers were running towards us, terrified. Someone among those who came was heard saying: "When you see all this it frightens you. You'd think it was the wrath of God." And old Zervoudákis murmured: "It's not enough that we're beaten down by poverty. We make it worse with our self-destruction, we foolish people who won't show any sign of coming to an agreement. We only want to strut about flattering ourselves that we're clever."

The bosses and the others began to show themselves. They came out of their houses, all of them hurt. Cockroach was lying on the ground groaning. They had crippled him. Big boss, Stávros had been badly beaten up. They rushed him to the hospital. A stone had hit him near the temple, and he was in danger. The gendarmes were searching for their caps and pistols. None of them had their pistol. They had thrown them away out of fear. They hadn't hurt us children. They had only given Liólios a vicious kick and he was going to his house limping and gasping with pain.

"Were you afraid for your son too?" someone derisively asked my mother. "Who would lift a hand to *him*? He's half-dead already." My mother ignored this. She held me tightly by the hand and was taking me home as if she were holding a treasure.

THE IDYLL

A family came to settle in our neighbourhood. For a short time they had lived at Mrs. Vasílaina's house, three or four doors down from where we lived. They had two daughters, one of them called Koúla who had just begun to walk and the other called Katína, who was seven or eight years old, the same age as me. She had fair hair and delicate features, and with long eyelashes framing her big blue eyes which looked glamorous. She always wore shoes and a clean dress. Her appearance made a great impression among us bare-footed ragamuffins. When we played school we made Katína be the teacher. She liked that. She wanted to improve us. After we finished the songs and the poems our teacher Katína would say to us: "You must wash your face, your ears, your hands, and your feet!"

One time as we were sitting playing school, Katína took my foot, looked at it carefully and said: "They've got very dirty." I hadn't any shoes. My mother wasn't able to buy them for me and I went about all year barefoot. In the winter, when I went out in the frost the skin on my feet would crack and they bled. These cracks became small wounds and sometimes they would run with pus. In the summer, with the heat, the wounds healed and the scabs would disappear, but no matter how much I washed them with hot water and soap, the scars remained and my feet looked dirty all the time.

When we played weddings and baptisms the children would make Katína and myself husband and wife in a marriage ceremony. They handed out roasted chick-peas for sugared almonds and there were songs and dances. Then Katína and myself as husband and wife would go a bit away from everyone and sit side by side, as we thought the adults did. I don't remember that we said anything but we would gaze at each other sitting there, and our eyes would say the sweetest words that had ever been spoken.

There were many boys in our neighbourhood. I saw Níkos Kolokoúris as a rival for Katína. He was the most handsome of us all. Very egoistic, he boasted a lot, and that took away from his attraction. Zervoudákis used to take me with him in his gig to the neighbourhoods where he sold his vegetables. I felt worried about going far away from Katína yet I couldn't tell Zervoudákis I wasn't going with him. The work I did for him was worth my while. Zervoudákis would pare and clean with his penknife an overripe fruit, a fresh broad bean, a stick of celery, a cauliflower, or broccoli and give it to me to stave off my hunger. I would pull off an outer leaf of a vegetable to throw into my ever empty stomach.

The whole day I went about with Zervoudákis I would pass the hours thinking about her. I would imagine her passing by and talking to me and looking at me with those marvellous eyes. When something happened that dragged me away from my beautiful dream I didn't feel good. I was impatient to get back to it.

Life was very beautiful at this time. If I was barefoot and ragged it didn't hinder me in any way, nor did I think about it.

One afternoon, when I was returning with Zervoudákis from the "district" as he called the area he traded in, the sun was still high and people were coming and going.

Among them I could see Katína and Níkos talking. I felt deeply hurt. When we came near, Níkos had gone. She called out to me happily: "Panayótis, you've come back."

I was abashed and didn't reply. This always happened to me when we were alone: I was not able to speak to her nor look at her directly.

Shortly after, I went to her yard. I felt a great need to see her. We played all our games there and it was covered with cement. In our neighbourhood there was no cement anywhere else and in our houses we had earthen floors. I hadn't been in her yard before without other children. It was deserted. I strolled around it and stood at the well. I looked in. The water shone down there like a window-pane. The thought occurred to me: "If I jump in so what? One jump and it's all over." I don't know if I would have carried out this idea. Yorghía Zervoudákaina came and pulled me away by the hand and said very angrily: "Get away from the well. If it was any other child I'd give him a good beating." I was grieved at her behaviour. In the neighbourhood they didn't scold us. They pitied us for having no father.

Yorghía was a beautiful girl, two or three times older than me. I had a romantic relationship with her. I would gather flowers in the fields and bring them to her. As soon as I saw her passing by I would stop and sing to her. She called me her "little boy". She married a White Russian called Vania and betrayed me. I had other such luckless romances with older girls. They would get married and betray me. Years later I got on very well with their daughters as my girlfriends.

Fellow-countrymen of the groom were brought to Yorghía's wedding. They had with them balalaikas, accordions, violins, and other instruments. Our poor neighbourhood was filled with happy tunes.

Everybody was gathered there. I didn't go too near. I had been very grieved that they were taking Yorghía from me but I just couldn't leave; the music held me. Without realising I found myself mingling with the others. Apart from the music, Nina, the most beautiful girl in the neighbourhood, was also attracting me there. I admired and respected her as any beautiful thing inspires respect and love. Wherever she was she stood out. She was always smiling as if she too were conscious of her charms.

As she led the dance she would make little coquettish and playful movements. She knew she was admired. She was friendly and spoke to everyone. When any man behaved slyly towards her she would turn from him and go away.

They were playing magical waltzes on the instruments. They also sang one of them:

> *Now you are leaving*
> *You fly to another*
> *And break your vows*
> *And me you forget*

Should the sun fade away
And the moon disappear
Only then I'll reject
A heart that I love.

This song enchanted me; it also made me cry inconsolably. "It's lovely to be a child," I heard someone say, "to love what you see, to find joy in everything and carry it all with you in fantasy, and to say now and again that life is beautiful." In the evening, when we gathered together to play weddings and baptisms, the children said they would marry Katína to Níkos. She looked straight at them as if she was surprised at their decision and said sulkily: "I don't want to !" She came and stood beside me and held my hand tightly. *I* wouldn't dare to do that. I saw that girls mature more quickly than boys. Níkos was barefoot too, as we all were. He wore unpatched trousers and a new coloured shirt. It looked very well on him, only that he spoiled it by wearing a neckerchief as the adult tough guys did. He also boasted exaggeratedly. From then on Katína was acknowledged as my wife.

One time I got hold of two corn cobs. I was very happy that I had something to offer Katína. I chose the bigger one for her and started planning how I would stretch out my hand to give it to her. When I finished the rehearsals I thought about what I would say to her.

On other occasions too I had made an attempt to tell her what I felt about her. I never managed to say anything. "Now," I told myself, "you must succeed since you're giving her such a big gift." The value of the gift kept increasing in my eyes. I was walking around outside her door, intoxicated with happiness. I was burning with impatience. When would Katína come out so that my uncontrollable joy would be realised.

At some moment, before I became aware of it, she came out and cried: "Panayótis, where are you going?"

I got confused. I always got confused in front of her and I couldn't speak to her. This time I was trembling. It felt as if I was preparing something bad for her and she caught me in the act.

"Panayótis, what's that you're holding? Corn cobs? Give me one!" she said with delight, and with the certainty that I wouldn't refuse her. My dreadful stage-fright made me not able to give it to her. And when she went away, and I was left with the corn cobs in my hands, I felt a great sadness. Decades have gone by since then. I didn't see her again. But when I remember that I didn't give her the corn cob I still feel sorry. There are even times when I weep.

THE FLOOD

Since night time there had been terrible thunder and lightning. In the morning, when it was still dark, the storm broke out. Our girls got up to go to work.

"Where are you going? God's destroying the world out there," said my mother in a frightened voice.

My sister Eléni opened the door and closed it at once. Very alarmed she said: "The rain's coming down from the heavens in rivers." Our roof was leaking everywhere. They put down the washtub, the boiler, the cooking pot, and the basin; whatever we had we set them down here and there to catch the drips. My mother moved about very agitated, picking us up, gathering up the clothes, and the straw mattresses that were on the floor, and had begun to get wet with the rain falling from the roof. She put us four young ones on the divan and threw over us an old patchwork blanket that we used as a bed-covering.

"If rain pours in on us here what will we do with the children? The walls are cracked from the flood last year," said my mother and she peered at the walls, reaching for the old cracks with her almost sightless eyes.

Her eyes had been injured when she was whitewashing a wall in a house where she worked as a charwoman. When she was up on the ladder one of the steps broke and she fell off. The lime was freshly slaked. It got into her eyes, making one of them useless, and with the other she could see very little. It took her months to recover. She was groaning and crying day and night with the pain.

My mother was also in the habit of crying at the slightest thing. A woman neighbour said once: "She cries a lot. The poor woman's afraid she won't be able to carry the burden of such a large family."

"Let's take the children to Mrs Hrístaina," said our Eléni. Hrístaina had a stone-built house with some steps up to it. Eléni took me on her back and opened the door. The water was roaring fiercely outside. It was flowing swiftly by, turning hither and thither, coming up to the rim of the door, ready to leap in. My sister quickly closed the door again and left me on the divan.

"The river has surrounded us. What are we to do!" she whimpered, very frightened. Water started to come in the door.

My mother and my sisters were trying to stop it. They filled in the chinks in the door with rags, but when they closed one hole another would open. The water was pushing against the door about to fling it down. Suddenly they stopped trying to hold the water back. The room had become a lake. The river had opened a hole in the brick wall. The water surged violently in and immediately reached the divan. Athanasía opened the door and wailed: "Aah my God we're lost! Help us. It's a sea in here." I hadn't ever seen the sea and I was longing to see it. The way I saw it now I didn't like it; I was afraid of it. My mother and sisters were standing with the muddy water above their knees and were crying. Eléni made her way to the door and shouted again and again: "Help, help! We're drowning!" Outside it wasn't raining any more. The river had swept away the little kitchen and the fence that separated Mrs Ventoúraina from us. Yórghis Ventoúris and his father came and brought us to their house, putting their own lives in danger.

The Ventoúrises took an interest in us. The greatest interest was shown by Yórghis who aspired to be Eléni's bridegroom. He served for a while as a stoker on a ship. One time when he came home on leave he gave my sister a piece of cheese; it was a hard, overripe cheese, dark on the outside and I still haven't forgotten the taste of it.

When the water receded we went outside to find that the fences and the small kitchens in the neighbourhood had all been utterly ruined. The houses looked graceless on their own. They were holding onto one another as if they were dead drunk. The muddy water that had flowed past left thick mud behind. The whole place had become unrecognisable and ugly. I couldn't bear to look at it. When I went outside a dreadful dampness chilled me through. I couldn't believe that this was where we lived. I felt I was there temporarily and something inside me was urging me to leave. I was frightened when I saw the place changing so quickly and our lives being instantly shattered. In one part, where a river was forming, adults, wading in muddy water rising high around them, were gathering things covered in mud, such as tables, chairs, cradles, trunks, washbasins, cauldrons, blankets, sheets, dresses, trousers, undershirts, and underpants. Among other things, Zervoudákis caught hold of a little baby in swaddling clothes.

"Don't bury it in a graveyard. It won't have been baptised," said Katrabasoú, a renowned professional mourner from Máni.

Fánis, who was a well-digger, dug a grave for the baby. When he was lifting the baby to take it and bury it he slid his arm under its little back and legs. "Look at how he's holding it," a little girl commented, "the way mothers lift them when they're sleeping."

"This one's sleeping never to wake up," said Mrs Antónaina, her words drowned in tears.

Mrs Antónaina had no children. She had had one but it died as a baby, and when she caressed someone else's child, she would remember her own and weep inconsolably. From time to time she would come over to us children where we were playing and give us a few coins for the soul of her child. In her hand she would be holding a handkerchief, wet with tears.

To Zervoudákis the grave didn't look deep enough. "Fáni, go down a bit more so that the dogs don't dig it up." Fánis put the child down, went into the grave and continued to dig silently. Shortly Zervoudákis glanced into the hole and said: "That's enough, drop it in." Fánis came out, took the child, knelt down and dropped it into the grave. A squirt of muddy water flew up and dirtied his face.

"The child's full of water like a flask," said Fánis as he wiped his face with the inside of the tail of his jacket. After staying silent for a moment, he lit a cigarette and murmured: "I'm ready for the grave and I came out of it and put in the child who isn't ready for it. How can life be like this?"

We didn't find out if the baby was a boy or a girl. With the flood everyone had their own misfortunes and didn't concern themselves with the baby. Then after a day or two I heard Noákaina saying to Fánis: "Did you not unswaddle it to untie its little hands and free them? It'll go to the other world to stand in front of them like a robber with bound hands."

"Don't upset yourself," Fánis replied. "They're all bound in the other world. If they left them unbound they would come back; nobody would want to stay. Even those few men and women who went of their own will, if we were able to ask them there, they would tell us they regret it."

Mítros suffered a great catastrophe. The water pulled down his house, swept away the fence and drowned all the goats. Most of them were carried off by the water; they couldn't be found anywhere. Some that were around, half-concealed by the mud, he dragged to the plot which used to be an animal fold, and he kept them lying there for several days. "Poor, unfortunate Mítros hasn't the heart to bury them," said Vasílis.

When days had passed and the mud had dried, everyone began to put their lives in order again. They fenced the yards in whatever way they could. One would bring stones and build a stone wall with them; another would bring tins and dig up some dry earth to fill them with and set them out in a row; most people gathered the mud that the river had brought with it, and threw in some straw and kneaded it to make mud bricks. With these they repaired the damage and gradually the neighbourhood took on its former appearance.

NEOCHRISTIANS

When Hrístos Flitsákos, who worked as a conductor on the Power trams, saw them building the fences he approached them, put his large stick firmly onto the ground and leaning heavily on it began to speak in his native Máni accent: "Health and strength to you, neighbours. I see you're fencing everything. You don't want it to be all one, so that there's no yours and mine, and your love can go out and spread and it can be as Christ taught, that we open our hearts and we all become one."

Old Liás, who was half-blind, said: "Let our hearts be open, but close our doors."

Flitsákos spoke again: "Christ had nothing of his own. His teaching was about love, common interest, common joy, common suffering . . . "

"Neighbour, Christ had no children and didn't need anything. We who have children want everything. And if I leave my door open, the other one will close his," said Mavrídis, a thin man. From bad habit he kept one eye closed which made you think he *had* actually lost it. Rarely did he open it. It was fearfully angry at being closed in, like a prisoner, and when you were speaking to him and saw it open, you shuddered; it was so frightening.

"Yes, neighbour, he closes the door," replied Flitsákos, "because he sees *our* doors closed. We have to begin with ourselves. We'll open our own hearts and spread our love, and our love will attract the love of the other to us."

One day Mavrídis said: "Flitsákos has his own psalter, tedious and incomprehensible. He talks about a change. We have to destroy families, pull down churches, throw out the priests and have no saints. He carries far too many books. It's those that are making him an atheist."

The people in the neighbourhood were illiterate and looked upon books with disapproval. They avoided Flitsákos. They considered him dangerous. And there were other fellow countrymen of his from Máni who worked on the trams. They would gather secretly in houses and have discussions. Once, as they were going along in ones and twos, for this purpose old Hrístos Vendoúris said: "Look at them going to their discussions like the first Christians to the meeting-place."

"These aren't Christians," replied Yánnis Kapetanákis whose tall stature made people listen to him. "They don't believe in *our* Christ. They have their own, somebody called Lenin. They call *him* Christ, the fraudulent Christ, the false Christ. They mix him up with ours and turn the world upside down. They've confused the people so that they don't know what's happening to them . . ."

Among those in the neighbourhood who regarded Flitsákos and his companions with hostility because of their ideas, some eventually agreed with them and became their fanatical followers.

Along the railway line that was close to us they had covered the telegraph poles with photographs of Lenin. When I was passing there I thought the red colours were very striking and I stopped to look at the photos.

A young boy from the neighbourhood, who was older than me, ran over to me and pulled me away: "Come here you. You shouldn't look at these photographs," he said to me, very frightened.

From the way he said it I thought I had done something bad and his fear transferred itself to me. I followed him, feeling scared. When we approached the houses he went off and left me without giving me an explanation. I was left alone to ponder the mystery. Who will punish me? The police, the people, God? What I couldn't explain was, to what was I doing harm and what harm was there in looking at a photograph. My small brain couldn't sort it out. After that, when I happened to pass that way I walked by quickly with beating heart and didn't lift my eyes to the photographs. They stayed there for a while until they were destroyed by the rains. Then, in the evenings, as soon as it got dark, there could be heard in the neighbourhood soft, timid voices, full of mystery: "The Leader, the Leader." When you heard these voices you thought there was something in them. A message was coming from a distant, unknown, fantastic world.

Flitsákos had one daughter and three sons. He had named one of the sons Lenin. We children couldn't say it like that. We called him Lení as his mother did. His father singled him out. He cared for him more than for his other children. "See how he looks on that child," said old Hrístos Vendoúris.

"You would think his life hung on that child. It's as if he was expecting something great from him."

Apart from Flitsákos and his companions, from time to time a neochristian from outside would appear in the neighbourhood. One Sunday, someone came, gathered together the older children and spoke to them. They chased us young ones away. "Eh, go away children. Wait till you're a bit older," said Thomás and stretched himself up to make his short stature taller by a centimetre. At first Thomás's family had goats. He was an awkward shepherd. He had a country accent and he spoke quickly. They couldn't understand him and used to tease him. The business with the goats didn't go well and they stopped it. Thomás went and started work elsewhere with a relative.

He immediately wore a hat and was smitten with the desire to act the big fellow. At first they made fun of him. He continued to wear the straw hat. Gradually they got used to him, so they left him alone, but he didn't stop speaking in a country accent and they laughed at him as before.

When the speaker left, the young people who had heard him looked pleased. "Look at the way they're acting. As if they've been eating sweets," said Antónis Vendoúris who was my age. He went to school. He could read and write and was clever.

Shortly after that, Drakoúlis Marghiólis came up to us. He looked at us in a friendly way and said to me: "*You* could have been there to hear him." But it wasn't possible; others were standing close by.

"Did you need our weight to bring you down?" asked

Antónis. "Don't you know you've sunk on your own without us?"

It was said that when Thomás left the neochristianizer, never having been to this kind of religious service before, he went home, got up on a chair and shouted: "Mother, come and help me take down the icons. I want to dust them."

When they took them down Thomás brought them out into the yard, set fire to them and burned them.

Next day at the furnace there was widespread discussion about the itinerant christianizer. As soon as I arrived I heard the boss saying to Pisadákis: "So what did he say to you then? We must be baptised as adults like Christ so that we know our godfather? He wasn't a good man; he was a rogue. That's the way they start. First they catch on to religion. They say, by the way, that they're following what Christ said, that they're applying his teaching properly. These people, you know, the police are pulling them in," said the boss, looking searchingly in the eyes of those children who had heard the "Christian", as if he wanted to know if his words frightened them as he expected.

"Tell me, what was he like? What did he wear?" the boss again asked Stéfanos who had heard the speaker. Stéfanos looked very scared and answered unwillingly: "He was a handsome man, well-dressed in a new suit, tie, suede shoes, trilby, and .. a red carnation in his lapel."

"Ah, so," said the boss, smiling ironically. "He had a red carnation in his lapel!"

When the boss went off Pisadákis commented: "Did you notice? He thought the red carnation had significance but avoided saying clearly what it was. If he had said it would have opened our eyes."

THE HUMAN AND THE INHUMAN

We stayed for a few days at Ventoúraina's house. All our belongings were covered with mud. My mother and sisters took everything out of the house, shook the muddy straw out of the sacking cloth mattresses and washed them. The house had become dangerous. The cracks on the wall had widened, one side had tilted inwards and some people expressed their misgivings. "It'll fall." "It's dangerous. It won't hold up. Don't go in. It'll trap you under it," said Mr Vasílis who had the voice of authority.

Our girls, in their bare feet, carried the mud out in buckets, cleaned the house and opened the window and the door. They left open the hole that the river had made so as to let in some air and dry the house quickly. Soon the owner of the house arrived. She looked carefully around inside, closed the window, locked the door, took the key, and started to walk away. My mother ran in front of her. "What are you doing, Mrs Kóstaina?" she asked, terrified.

"What am I doing? You ask me what I'm doing? I've locked the house and taken the key. I built the house with blood and tears. It's not possible for you to live here with six months' rent not paid. I have a family too. My son Yorghís is ill and I can't afford to buy him medicine," said the house-owner angrily.

"Mrs Kóstaina, haven't we paid you for so many years? We'll give you the money later. As you see I haven't earned anything for such a long time. You know that accursed white-wash blinded me."

"I can see that the whitewash has blinded you and you won't be able to find work easily to pay me the rent, to give me my money."

"In the name of God, have pity on us. Think what will become of us."

We young ones waited in anguish. My sisters, who hadn't had time to wash themselves, were standing in front with their legs covered with mud above their knees. They were bent down, lifting the hems of their dresses and wiping their tears.

"I can't, I can't, don't beg me," said the houseowner in exasperation. "I want the rent you owe me; I'm not asking you to lend me money. I'm going to build the fence and the kitchen."

"Mrs Kóstaina," said my mother, weeping, "we haven't any money now. Wait just a little. We'll give it to you later on. If we don't give it to you, do what you like with us. Make us your slaves."

"What are you saying, Mítsaina," she shouted, even more exasperated. "Are you out of your mind? I can't support my own family that I'm saddled with. Am I going to burden myself with yours too?"

My mother implored the houseowner. Weeping, she fell at her feet. We young ones began to cry. Our sisters were crying too. She wasn't moved in the slightest. In the yard she had other one-room houses that she let out. One of them, the biggest, which had windows looking onto the street, was rented by us at first. When my father died and my brothers went away we weren't able to pay the rent. We left that house and the seven of us huddled into the small one.

We had come into this house when I was still very young. I knew it as our first home. I could tell with my eyes closed where each dent or hole was on the wall, and the cracks, the swollen plaster ready to fall, the parts that had collapsed and that my mother had repaired with a paste of mud and straw, using the palm of her hand.

My mother, whose eyes had not stopped flowing with tears, took me by the hand and we went off.

Each time my mother or my sisters went out somewhere, they took one of us young ones with them. They didn't bring us along to beg. Our presence had quite another purpose. They wanted us for their own protection. The weakness of a young child was the strength that protected them. This time my mother didn't take me for that reason. I realised she was taking me with her for something else, which grieves me even now when I remember it. She took me so that the boss would see me as the security she was relying on for him to give her money.

I was ashamed, but what could I have done; we were without a home. It was days since I had been at work. The water that had flowed through the furnace had done great damage to the unfired bricks. The boss had ordered us not to come to work until the mud was well dried and then he would call us.

When we came into the furnace and my mother saw how the river had wrecked the place a deathlike disappointment spread over her face. She turned pale. I was afraid when I saw her like this. I said to myself: "She'll fall and never get up again." I began to cry and couldn't stop. "Don't cry little one," said my mother who didn't realise why I was crying. "People's hearts are sore when they see great disasters like this happen in the world."

Her words consoled me. I saw that her morale had not completely gone. From the start, when I set off with my mother to see the boss, I felt something tense inside me, and as we drew nearer to meet him, I felt the tension increasing. And at any moment when the boss would come and not give us the money I thought the tension would snap and hit me on the heart and I'd die on the spot.

In the shed where we went about a dozen men were working and old Apostólis as well. As soon as he saw us, he came to us. I was pleased. I wanted my mother to meet the man I had told her so many good things about. If someone else had come, I would have been worried. He might have made scathing comments about her, for a laugh, as they were accustomed to doing, even though my mother was in a pitiful state. "What happened? The rain did you some damage?" Apostólis asked.

"The rain has come and gone, my good man, and we're left without a home," said my mother and her tears flowed.

She related the whole piteous story to Apostólis. I felt ashamed; I didn't want them to know that we were in such a terrible plight.

Apostólis was pale and skinny, and as he was listening to my mother he closed his eyes as if he hadn't the heart to see the light of this beautiful day revealing such a great calamity before him. He said: "When the boss hears this, he ought to give you some money. Out of the damage that you see he has suffered, he'll make many times more money. In all the furnaces the unfired bricks were damaged in the flood, and they've stopped production. There'll be a great shortage of them; the millions of bricks our boss has in piles already fired he'll sell for twice the price or even more. If he doesn't give you anything I'll tell the others and we can have a collection among ourselves."

"A thousand blessings on you, a thousand blessings," said my mother with great relief, and she bent down to kiss his hand. He pulled it quickly away as if she were going to insult him. But for my mother it was an expression of gratitude, as it generally is with the humble when anyone does good to them. Besides it was for her the first encouraging words she'd heard in the midst of her dreadful despair.

The word "collection" that Apostólis said he would arrange with the other workers struck me to the heart. I knelt down and clung onto my mother's skirts as if I wanted to hide, to go away from him, and bury myself somewhere. I couldn't bear such a blow.

At that moment my life seemed nothing to me; I could have smashed it as if it were a mere toy. I knew very well how poor they were and I couldn't accept that we should take the bread from the hungry children of these men. "Here he is now. He's coming down," said Apostólis and he slowly moved off to go back to his work.

The boss came into the shed and pretended he didn't see

us. He must have understood why we had come and didn't approach us. He moved farther away where Manólis Kopsós was sitting.

When my mother saw that he was avoiding us she looked overwhelmed with disappointment and stood as still as if she were lifeless.

"Come here," Kopsós called to us. As the boss's cousin he could behave with more independence at work. When we were walking over to Kopsós, my mother held me close to her. It was obvious that she was leaning on me for support, like someone with a crutch.

When we were standing in front of him, my mother said "Good-bye" in a choking voice. I had learned that we say "good-bye" when we're leaving, and I pitied my unhappy mother who, in her confusion and despair, became muddled. The boss, who was listening, smiled ironically. He took my unfortunate mother's mistaken greeting for ignorance. It's painful to me remembering it even now.

"Sit down, woman dear," Kopsós said to her, pointing to some bricks made up as a seat. My mother sat hunched up on the bricks and as she was thin and poorly dressed she looked like a rag doll in the arms of a poor child. "What's the matter? The water came into your house?" asked Kopsós. My mother again related our great calamity. As she was ending her story she gulped with nervousness and said to the boss: "Mr Pandelís, I've come to ask you if you could give us an advance payment, whatever it would please you to offer. And when the children work you can keep their wages. I would be indebted to you as long as I live."

At the words "advance payment" the boss looked satisfied. From the moment he saw us he had an idea that we had come for money, and when he heard it from my mother's lips he smiled because it didn't fall short of his expectation.

I didn't like this. I had heard that many people don't care even if they lose money as long as they are proved correct in their expectations and their contemptible, egotistical instinct is satisfied. My mother was telling her story and it was clear that she was suffering. And as one of her eyes was closed and was completely ruined, and the other was half open and clouded and she could scarcely see with it, the boss looked at her rather with contempt, and said indifferently: "What do you want me to do? Who hasn't got troubles? As you see, the river took thousands of bricks from me. Now the rains are getting worse; we're coming into winter. The work will stop soon. How many days' work will your children do from now on? What kind of money can I give you that they will be able to pay back?"

"You know yourself boss. Give what you think. I'm putting my hope in you and in God," said my mother and her tears flowed again. My heart was sinking. I couldn't bear any more. It was two days since I had put anything in my mouth, like all of us.

"Pandelís, give a hundred drachmas from me and you can keep it on Saturday," said Kopsós and his lips twitched nervously.

Kopsós had regular work. He earned the highest wage and was paid overtime at night. He didn't do any work with his hands. He had two helpers and he only supervised them. He was not without his needs as well. He had four children. At midday, when his wife would bring him food, one of them, little Eléni would follow at her heels and before her mother arrived she would run and be there first. "What have we brought you today, papa?" she would ask, laughing with delight. Her father would look into her eyes and repeat: "We have—we have—we have—potatoes!"

"Ah, you've guessed it again!" the little girl would shout, laughing and clapping and making coquettish gestures. When she calmed down she would throw herself on him and say: "Dear papa, how do you guess?"

"A little bird comes and tells me, my pet. Apart from the bird, your beautiful eyes tell me."

"My eyes? Tomorrow I'll close them!"

The evening before, Kopsós would talk to his wife about the food she would make for him. The next day the little girl put her hand over her eyes and asked charmingly: "What have we for you today, papa? Come on tell me, tell me, quick. I'm not joking."

I was captivated by that child. But she made me remember that I hadn't a father.

The boss said to Kopsós: "Leave it, Manólis. I'll give a hundred drachmas and I'll make a note of them as advance payment."

"Apart from your hundred, that you're giving as advance payment, cousin, add a hundred from me. I want to give it to them," Kopsós said. At this point we couldn't help ourselves; my mother and I cried loudly. I could see that sometimes kindness makes you cry more than a beating would.

The boss frowned, bent his head, took a bundle of notes from his pocket and gave my mother two hundred drachmas.

Kopsós stroked his brown moustache from one side to the other and said: "I have suffered misfortune too. My father didn't die. His spirit was broken by our poverty. He was a young man when he died because he hadn't enough to feed us . . ."

When he stopped speaking he stayed motionless. He looked uncanny. All of him had emptied away. It was as if he had gone from us, had become nothing, a zero; as if his distant past had swallowed him up.

I saw how quickly a person can die. It was as if I knew all of life and its end, as if I heard Kopsós speaking in a short fairy-story and only these words stayed with me: "My father didn't just die. His spirit was broken by our poverty." When Kopsós returned from his momentary journey his face had changed as one would see it years later. He looked as if he had come from a place where life had not gone well for him, where his soul had been tormented.

"His spirit was broken by our terrible poverty," he said once again. It was like a moan that his unjustly lost father was sending from the distant past.

My mother thanked them a thousand times and we left. I stopped by with Apostólis and told him what happened. On the way home I felt light as if a heavy burden had gone from me. I couldn't bear to see my mother in such a dreadful situation. I couldn't bear for her to suffer so many calamities and, whether she had the courage or not, to have to tell about them, to recount her tragedy in every small detail in order to move people so that they would pity her and give her money. I could see that it was necessary to inspire this emotion so that they would be willing to give something to her, but here, she wasn't giving a performance or reading from a book. It was her life, her real suffering that she should have forgotten in any way she could. She told about her suffering and was choking with distress. She was choking in the telling of it, by her own hands, so as to convince others that she really was in distress.

WITH MONEY THE SUN COMES OUT

The houseowner took the money and handed over the key, all smiles. Having seen her so angry before, I thought she would never be able to calm down and give us the key to get into the house. When she was given the money, she suddenly changed. She stroked my mother's skinny back, which must have made her shudder, and said: "Mítsaina, we're like sisters. One minute we fall out and the next we make it up. We never part."

I had noticed that the houseowner always called my mother, Mítsaina and my mother called her Mrs Kóstaina. It would not have befitted her to call my mother Mrs Mítsaina, which showed that she saw my mother as her poor, inferior tenant and this distressed me. When the houseowner took her large bulk off, away from us a bit, she put on her glasses and unfolded the notes again that my mother had given her. Motionless and smiling, she looked at them for a long time. You wouldn't have thought she was that harsh woman who threw us out of the house. I just couldn't believe it. I saw once again how all-powerful money is, how it changes a person so quickly that you simply can't believe it.

"What's she looking for in those notes?" said Proferákos about the houseowner who he saw looking at the notes with so much devotion. "Maybe she wants to see the drama a person has to go through to acquire it, and how fast he loses it? Or, she doubts if it's genuine since whatever happens around here seems false to her."

The house became spick and span. They filled the sack-cloth mattresses with dry straw and they threw plenty of straw on the floor to absorb the damp. We were all happy. We young ones couldn't control ourselves; we did somersaults and jumped about and wrestled and danced. We went crazy. To the girls this was something new.

"What a joy it is to get back what we had before and lost!" said Hrístaina, smiling as she watched us, leaning against our door-frame.

The boss summoned us back to work. On the first day we went back, we heard that Níkos the Goldfinch had died. Nikólas, who had gone to the funeral, said: "He couldn't bear the humiliation. He was a sensitive lad. He was wounded to the heart and died." He paused for a moment and then continued: "Níkos's father was crying out fit to break your heart: 'He was my only child. His mother died and I brought him up. He was the greatest joy of my life. To have him alive—I would work day and night for him just to have him alive so that I could see him.'"

I remembered that Níkos, when the boss struck him, went away a little distance from the furnace and sat down, put his head on his knee and wept. Where he had bent over, the ground was dyed with his blood for days. I wept for his death. I couldn't believe he had died. I thought I would see him at work. I would hear his voice in my head and his beautiful singing. I thought he would call to me: "Troubadour, you fantastic child."

He passionately loved singing. When we were eating he would give voice and sing one or two verses. When he stopped he would explain: "It's from Rigoletto by Verdi."

The other workers would make fun of him and laugh. He would laugh with them. Once Aléxis Skamángas, who was a boorish joker, said to him: "Goldfinch, why don't you bring your composer here and we'll squeeze him in with us at the kiln and he can take the hot bricks with his bare hands as we do?"

Níkos would often mention the names of composers. Everyone showed deep sorrow at his death. Now and again they would say: "The poor lad, gone for nothing! What a fine young man, what a face and figure he had, what a kind heart! And he always had a smile."

"And his voice, he sang so beautifully. He had an artistic talent," said Stéfanos.

Stéfanos was ugly. He had big ears, thick lips, a large mouth and a rough, unattractive voice. I was sorry that nature had been so unfair to him.

Stéfanos and I worked together for a time. He was always doing good. When he had a morsel of bread he would cut it in half and give it to someone who didn't have any. He was polite and self-respecting and always told the truth. No ugly word ever came out of his mouth. He always spoke kindly. I admired him and would go to him all the time. I sought to resemble him.

One time Stéfanos went to a furnace far away. During a

conversation his fellow-workers were having about him one day at break-time, someone remarked: "He's good, but he's very ugly." Another one answered: "He's ugly, but he is good.", and kindness doesn't need beauty; beauty needs kindness." When they said a good word about Stéfanos I was as pleased as if it had been about me. I always had it in mind to go and find him. One day I decided to go, and set off on the road there. When I came to the place where he worked, I found that his boss was an old man. When I told him about Stéfanos, he shook his head and said, in the slow way that elderly people speak: "It's years since Stéfanos left. Some-body took him abroad." I was stunned! "It's not long since I saw him," I said to my fellow-converser. "It's as if it was yesterday."

"Agh," the old man said slowly and feelingly. "The time goes quickly. It's like everything happened yesterday!"

I was grieved that I wouldn't see my friend any more and when I was returning home my heart was aching. I couldn't bear it. I wept as we would weep for someone who had died.

On Saturday, when we were being paid, the boss kept all the money earned by my brother and myself. I felt like a withered leaf. Our mother had told us to ask him if he would keep the half of it, and the rest of it the following week. I had undertaken this unpleasant task, and was about to say some-thing, but the boss scarcely let me open my mouth before he grabbed me by the arm, put me out of the office and said: "On your way, or I'll take a stick to you."

I hadn't the courage to go away. I went out and sat at the tank and gazed at the goldfish. The sight didn't attract me; I had seen it many times. After the boss had behaved badly to me, a blackness fell before my eyes and I couldn't see.

I was in despair. When the boss finished paying the others and came out, he saw me and called to me: "Little Tranoúlis, come and we'll see what to do with you."

I heard the mild tone in his voice as though he hadn't thrown me out roughly just before. I leapt up and found myself in front of him. "Sing me a song first and then we'll talk." He saw my reluctance and muttered: "All right, leave it for another time." He behaved as if it didn't matter but he looked serious. The corners of his mouth fell in an ugly grimace, showing that my reluctance had cut him to the quick. He took a piece of paper and wrote something on it. "Take this note. Your wages come to ninety-seven drachmas. I gave you a hundred when you were with your mother. You owe me three. Take seventeen more and you'll owe me twenty. Now off you go."

He said this to me in a very harsh tone. I knew he was behaving like this because I didn't sing for him. He wanted to remind me, in case I forgot, that he had authority over me. When I showed the money to my mother she looked at it sideways, as people do whose eyes are injured, and she said: "So did you not ask him to give you some more?"

"She'll have been expecting me to bring more," I thought. "I asked him. He didn't give it to me."

"Agh, agh," she said, "those who want to give money don't have it and those who have money haven't their heart in the right place to give it."

I had never heard my mother speak like this before. When

I was younger I remember that before my father died, although she wasn't very talkative, she would laugh and sing. She often sang this song:

> *Brave lad, where did you find*
> *This young girl, the fair-haired girl from Pátra*

She sang very beautifully. They used to praise her for her ability to sing in tune and for her beautiful voice. What ever could have happened to that beautiful voice?

Our little Manólis fell seriously ill with peritonitis. He wasn't getting any better. The doctor had given him up. He didn't write any more prescriptions and from those he wrote in the beginning we took only one or two to the chemist; the others lay in the house. My mother didn't sleep night or day and she rarely put any food in her mouth. How did she endure it?

Aléxis Skamángas had a brother called Níkos who was Kopsós' assistant at work. He was a fine man with a kind heart. He had a wife and children but never complained about his poverty. As if he had taken it upon himself to console us in our anxiety and fatigue he would tell jokes and make us laugh.

One day Níkos said to me: "Tell me, is your girl pretty? What's she called?"

"Katína," I said without caring that I was very young. I loved her very much and I wanted to talk about her all the time. Furthermore Níkos had given us young ones the courage to talk to him as if he were the same age as us.

"Katína," he cried out and his eyes lit up. "A most beautiful name, congratulations!" he said, shaking my hand. "She'll be a lovely girl, I imagine. You're a handsome lad too."

I couldn't see where he found this handsome lad in me. I was permanently barefoot and ragged. Our hair wasn't cut evenly all the way round. It was let grow and I had a rich crop. At the back it hung in a tail low down on the neck. Our hair was cut with a razor so that there were no nits left at the roots. This didn't happen in our homes. From time to time a barber, who was mentally affected by his sufferings in life, would pass through the neighbourhoods with a hair clipper in his hand, calling out: "Ákouris for haircuts, good people!" When Ákouris came, it would be a feast-day.

The neighbourhood was roused by the shouts and the children would gather for a haircut. He cut our hair without payment, otherwise who knows where it would have reached. Whenever one of us children didn't stand still to have our hair cut, Ákouris would hit us on the head with the clippers and we would be covered with bumps—and sometimes we would bleed but who could complain! To cut our hair he would take us outside the neighbourhood. "Why do you do that? Why do you take them so far away?" Zervoudákis asked him.

"So that the lice don't remember where they came from and go back to your houses," the itinerant barber replied.

When Ákouris was late in coming through the neighbourhood our mothers became very concerned. They saw our hair getting long and were afraid of the lice. When it took him a long time to come, our houses were in danger, as if from a raging fire.

Whenever our mothers treated the itinerant barber to a coffee it was brewed from chickpea or barley. That was what most of the houses had. In the other few houses they would throw in a little bit of real coffee and they praised it for its good taste.

"I too loved a Katína when I was young," said Níkos thoughtfully. "She was very beautiful. I can see her now," he said in a choking voice, and it seemed to me that he had become a child again. "Why did you not marry her?" I asked. He was silent as if something was happening inside him and he couldn't continue. Then he said: "Let it be," and he went away with so much grief you would have thought he was going to weep and never stop. I had noticed that sometimes adults behaved like this and you would think they were hiding a tragedy inside them and they made you pity them and suffer with them and feel their pain.

Whenever Skamángas was looking after the fire down in the furnace, he would sing very beautifully, long drawn-out love songs. He sang all the verses with passion:

I'll go and find the dead . . .
Please, Háron, tell me . . .

Once Nikólas Retetángos flung open his long arms and shouted: "Hey, namesake, with you we get confused. We don't know what to think. One minute you have us laughing and the next we're weeping at your sad songs."

THE FAREWELL

One day in November, work at the furnace came to an end at noon. "Hey fellows, I think we should smoke a cigarette like brothers before we separate," Nikólas Retetángos suggested.

They all gathered in the shed, sat on the bricks, and lit cigarettes. "An excellent idea, Nikólas. Gathered together like this it's as if we're saying a prayer to the Unknown for something good to happen to each of us poor men," said Drakoúlis, and he looked around with his big eyes wide open as if he wanted to fit everything he saw into them and keep it for ever. I was surprised and stunned! Something beautiful was happening, something important, like a miracle that I was taking part in.

Níkos Skamángas said: "Moulders, shall we do something? Shall we each contribute a few drachmas and buy some wine and we'll drink and sing and dance for the farewell?" He looked at them all, and then stared straight ahead for a moment as if he was seeing something passing and continued: "Who knows if we'll live to meet again here."

"What do you see, Nick. Are we going to die?" asked Mathiós, a very strong young man. As he went to sit down he stretched out his hand and his muscular arm appeared from his torn sleeve. It made you believe that this fine upstanding young man would never wear out. I liked Mathiós. He spoke in a deep voice and called Níkos, "Nick".

"I'm not saying we're going to die but let's not forget that we will die," replied Níkos.

"For us poor people in winter, it's as if we're having a close fight with death," said Yánnis from Piraeus, a tall, dark-complexioned man about whom Goldfinch had said: "I'm sorry for Yánnis, walking here and back to Piraeus every day. He reminds me of the punished Sisyphus!"[1]

"How will we get through the winter barefoot and naked? How will we feed the children?" Tzanís murmured sadly. At first he had been a well-digger. One day I heard him saying: "I couldn't do that work any more. It made me unhappy. It seemed as if I was opening wounds in the body of the earth."

I couldn't bear to be near them. The smoke made my eyes sting, but more than that, their words stung me to the heart. At first, when they sat down, I thought I would hear wise things spoken; something important would happen. But they were talking in a depressing way, as if they were lamenting.

---

[1]Sisyphus—a Greek mythological figure. According to Homer he was "the most crafty of men". He was the founder and king of Corinth. When Zeus abducted Aegina, the daughter of the river-god Asopus, the latter complained to Sisyphus about her disappearance and Sisyphus offered to reveal what happened on condition that Asopus would give water to the citadel of Corinth. Zeus in fury sent Death for him but Sisyphus chained Death and then deceived the god Pluto and returned to life. When after many years he died and went to the Underworld, he was condemned by the Gods to roll a heavy stone up a hill and start all over again when it rolled down. Hence "a Sisyphean work" is endless and futile.

Gradually, I lost them in the smoke; it was as if they didn't exist there, as if they were nothing, a smoking log, burning to no purpose, and as if they were trying to unite in there into a single force with one strong heart to puff and blow, to make it blaze into flame and throw out light so that the place would become beautiful, and life would change.

They got up, shook hands and in a sad voice wished one another "a good winter" and "till we meet again", and one by one they went away.

Nikólas saw me standing apart and called me with his usual salutation: "Come here, friend." When I came over to him he lifted me high in the air in his gigantic arms and kissed me. When he put me down, he said to me: "Remember, you did your first job with us. Never forget that; it's important. Good-bye."

I could never make out what was so important about that. In time, what I did understand was that my life was bound up with theirs in this torturing work and that I suffered deeply. I stayed for a while where Nikólas had left me. I couldn't leave. I felt bad all alone. My heart was wrung. I began to cry as if I had lost them for ever and had become fatherless again.

As I was going home, another time came to mind when we were fellow-workers gathered together again and they talked about Níkos the Goldfinch. The atmosphere had become charged with emotion. Nikólas Retetángos said: "Brothers, as we are here now, let's have a minute's silence for our beloved fellow-worker whom we lost so early in his life." Nikólas's voice was very sad like the voice of the night bird mournfully calling to his lost brother, the screech owl.

When the minute's silence was over, we all had tears in our eyes.

WINTER WITHOUT WORK

When I went home I found my mother at the door, looking happy. "Come, come," she said to me, "Manólis is better."

When I went into the room I saw the child walking. His little face was translucent with weakness.

That child was saved as if by a miracle. One day my mother wanted to rub him down and she hadn't any alcohol. Then she remembered that one time she had bought ouzo to treat our uncle Thanásis and she had a little of it left. She began to rub him with it but he was wanting to drink it. "Come here, dear," my mother called, "he wants to drink the ouzo." When I went over to him, I saw the child crying and asking for the ouzo. My mother was in a quandary. "What'll I do? Shall I give it to him?" she said to me.

"How do I know, mother."

"They say that whatever a sick person's body demands that's the medicine he needs. Anyway, the doctor said he won't live. I think I'll give it to him and not have him dying without it and crying for it."

I had noticed that many poor people, hit hard by life, were easily resigned to the death of a sick person in their home, as if the terrible poverty and the torment they went through dulled the pain of bereavement. You would have thought death had become a habit with the poor; many were to be born in every house and many were to die. When anyone from a poor family became ill and the doctor said he wouldn't get well, but prescribed medicine for him, that person was looked upon as a burden. When they bought medicine, the healthy ones were being deprived of bread and were themselves in danger of becoming ill. And there wasn't room for a sick person in the houses of the poor. Nor was there anyone to look after him. They all had to be free to hurry out to work, to be able to get bread. But when the poor person died, his relatives wept sorely for him, something you didn't see elsewhere and wouldn't have expected from them. You would have assumed that death occurred because of some injustice they thought had happened when he was ill and they weren't able to take care of him as they should have. He departed this life with a grievance, and they felt guilty about this and also because he had met with such an unfortunate fate.

One time Ventoúraina leant her tall, thin body against our door as she was accustomed to do and said to my mother: "How much do you earn where you're working, Mrs Mítsaina?"

"What do I earn? How much money? They don't give us money, only an armful of green vegetables, or a cabbage or cauliflower at midday and in the evening when we stop work, some food and bread. I keep it and bring it to the children. Another woman who was working with me, a strong woman, not like me, asked the boss to give her some money too. He was so angry you'd have thought he'd eat her. He shouted at her: 'If you like it, you can stay. If you don't like it and you're looking for money too you can get out of here. For money I can get men begging me to take them on. I don't need trash like you.' "

When Ventoúraina went away I huddled in a corner and wept. "Why are you crying?" my mother asked me anxiously.

"For what they do to you at work and they don't even pay you."

"You're crying for that?" she asked. She turned round and looked at me with her half-sighted eye and sighed: "Agh, agh, I was like that when I was small. When I heard my parents talking about our troubles I would cry and many a time I wouldn't eat. The bread seemed to have blood on it from what they had shed until they brought it home. But what can we do? It's God's will."

I loved God but I couldn't understand why He wanted us to be hungry. I said this to a friend and he explained to me: "God loves us poor people very much and wants us to come to him quickly."

"Since he loves us and wants us to come to him quickly why didn't he keep us in heaven?" I asked. He looked at me silently for a moment and said: "He sent us to work for the rich who don't know anything about work, and gave them everything so that they won't suffer because he doesn't love them, and He will then ill-treat them in heaven."

On Sundays, when my sisters didn't work, they would take Alékos and myself and we'd go to the river of Kallirrói and gather pieces of coke from the rubble that they threw out of the gasworks. When my mother saw us returning, laden with coke, she would come running and take the sacks from us, saying: "God keep you, children! We don't have enough bread but let's at least have some warmth."

My mother needed warmth. We were in want of many things: bread, soap, matches, oil for the lamp, and other things. We were regularly without oil. Many evenings we went to bed without light. On one of the many nights that we had run out of oil and had gone to bed in the dark, the girls came back. Athanasía said, with grief: "Mother, we've come in tired from work. We're going to bed hungry. Could you not keep a little oil to let us see where to put our clothes?"

"My dear child, the oil's been finished for days. Yesterday evening we kept a little for you. What can I do about it? I was tired too when I came home from work. I was hungry too and I went to bed in the dark. Who can I tell this to? Shall I tell your father who left me and didn't take me with him?" She began to weep.

"Come now, mother dear. I don't know why I behaved like that," Athanasía said to her and went to her to kiss her hand, crying. Eléni began crying as well and then we young ones started. Since we hadn't eaten anything in the evening we took our fill of tears.

It wouldn't have been the oil that made Athanasía speak like that. It would have happened anyway, without her being aware of it, urged on as she was by our poverty which was now unbearable. It had made us sensitive and we would cry for no good reason. When something happened I could see that we drew closer together. Even when we grew up and had families the bond did not weaken. My sister, Athanasía said once to her husband and children: "I love my brothers and sisters more than I love you."

When my mother brought home the green vegetables for her day's work she would boil them and we would eat them without oil, which we didn't have to put on them. She shared out the cabbage, cauliflower and broccoli uncooked. When there was a surplus of vegetables we were delighted. The boss would give my mother a larger amount and we had a more generous helping.

The money our girls earned from their work at the tobacco factory amounted only to two or three days' bread for us, so we were all hungry. Once I heard my mother saying: "Oh Athanasía, the young ones were crying with hunger all night and they were saying in their sleep, without knowing it, 'I'm hungry. I'm hungry.'" From hunger and lack of oil we got scabies and sore eyes. In the mornings when it was still dark, my mother would light a fire with the coke we had gathered. She would boil camomile to open our eyes that were glued shut. She would wash our hands and feet and apply sulphur. When she finished that job she started on the scabies. When she had done with the scabies she tackled the lice. "Come Panayótis," she would call with the comb in her hand. I would bend over the brazier and she would begin the combing. I knew how many lice fell from my head by the crackling they made in the fire. When there were few I wasn't pleased. I couldn't explain this. Was it because I didn't enjoy hearing them crackle or because the rich crop in my hair was becoming less abundant? When my mother had freed us from the comb she started on herself. She put down a piece of paper to comb herself. She was afraid to do this over the fire in case it would catch her hair which was long. When she finished, she folded up the paper and threw it in the fire. So the fate of her lice was no different from the fate of ours. Sometimes she would praise the comb: "An excellent comb, it's thick and it's got sharp teeth. It goes in deep and clears away the lice from the scalp."

We had found it in the rubbish heap. We washed it with alcohol and put it to use. Before that comb we had another, a very fine one; my mother had been given it by her grandparents towards her dowry. People in the neighbourhood borrowed it and I was pleased that we were also able to do something good. One day during the rounds it was doing in the neighbourhood it lost its way and didn't come back to us.

We used to go round the rubbish heaps and always managed to find something: pieces of cloth for patches or buttons from rags. We didn't take any clothes to wear although some of them were in good condition. We were afraid that they might have come from people who had tuberculosis and we would be infected. Tuberculosis was rife and devastating.

After the lice my mother would start work on the bedbugs. What she couldn't fight were the fleas. They would bite and make off. We all had them. We were used to them. They didn't bother us too much; it was as if they were our tenants. And sometimes when we were ill and they wanted to give us an injection they would say: "Don't think about it. It's nothing. The needle'll sting you just like a flea."

The relatives had forgotten us. Our great poverty humiliated them. When they were asked if we were their relatives they would say they didn't know us. Only uncle Thanásis would come and see us from time to time. I heard that he had his own shoemaker's shop. One time he brought me a pair of tan shoes. As soon as I tried them on mother said quietly: "That's enough. Take them off. You'll ruin them and you'll be barefoot on Sundays and feast-days." I took them off but I haven't forgotten yet the longing I had to wear them longer. It was the first time I had ever put on shoes.

On Sunday I put them on and went to church. It was a long time since I had gone and everything looked more beautiful to me than ever before. The chandeliers, the candlesticks, the oil lamps, the icons—everything impressed me. Even the priest, who wasn't likeable seemed more sympathetic to me.

I went and stood on the right near children from the neighbourhood who were my own age. Níkos Zaharákos, who was dressed like a priest, served at the Altar and assisted the priest in chanting "The Lord have mercy upon us." He had a strong position in the church. He decided which boys would assist in the sanctuary and which would ring the bell. One Sunday he was seen having an argument with the parish priest whom he accused of paying him less than he should, and I was impressed by the power that he had.

When Zaharákos saw me in church he looked surprised and nodded at me to get out. He always put me out of the church because I was barefoot. I went to him and whispered in his ear: "I'm wearing shoes." He looked as if he didn't believe me. He bent his big head to verify it with his own eyes. When he saw the shoes his face fell as if they had severely rebuked him.

Apart from Zaharákos there was old Anéstis, a tall, thin man. He would also put me out of the church for being barefoot. He sold candles at the candle counter. Whenever I managed to sneak in, he would come where I was standing, grab me by the ear, bring me outside and say maliciously: "I told you. It's forbidden to come into church barefoot. Spawn of the devil!"

One time, during such a scene, old Alékos Tambákis the tanner from the island of Páros, a very pious man, was standing near. "You behave in the house of God as if you were in your own house! A poor man is not permitted by you even to worship. There's no place for him here," he said in a low voice that matched his low stature. Somebody else murmured: "They're throwing out the poor boy who hasn't any money and they can't benefit from him."

One Sunday, old Mrs Zervoudákaina gave me money to go and light a candle for her. She was ill and couldn't go. As soon as I went in the church door, old Anéstis stopped me: "Where are you going?" I told him what had happened. I showed him the money that I had, to light the candle. He stood thoughtful for a moment, as if he was placed in a difficult situation but he easily overcame the difficulty. He grabbed my hand, took the money and shouted threateningly: "Go away!"

MIDWINTER SWALLOWS

Uncle Thanásis, on his rare visits, never came to us empty-handed. He would bring pears, peaches, grapes, or a big watermelon. One time he brought us a bag of cherries. How delighted we children were! We jumped about like mad creatures. I couldn't remember that we had ever eaten cherries but I knew what they were. What made us go mad with delight was when we found a stem with two or three cherries on it. We hadn't the heart to separate these. We held them up in the air and gazed at them with insatiable joy. We had great fun hanging them on our ears and prancing about the room. For all our longing to eat them we controlled ourselves and played games with them as if to prolong our delight. One Sunday, uncle came to our house with a beautiful, well-dressed woman. He was carrying a big parcel. As soon as we saw him coming, we ran and leapt on him. When the welcome ceremony was over he said: "Say hello to your aunt Eléni." He presented his wife to us and seemed pleased to see her looking at us happily.

My uncle was quite old and used to complain to my mother that he was still unmarried. This was the first time we saw our new aunt. He looked happy to have found a partner. His wife sensed this and preened herself in her fur coat.

When we went into the house I cleared off. I was ashamed of the sorry state we were in. There wasn't a place for our new aunt to sit down. Our two chairs stood upright with difficulty and they had holes in the straw.

The divan on wooden trestles didn't hold up. We put it against the wall so that it wouldn't fall. The sacking-cloth mattress, all lumpy with the straw that didn't spread out evenly looked as if it was alive and walking. Then when we wanted to make it more comfortable and tossed it about, the straw would crumble and fill the house with dust. The bed-cover was an old patchwork blanket soiled by us children who used to jump on the divan with dirty bare feet. The divan was the domain of us young ones, so that the seven people could move about in the small room.

Outside was no more comfortable; our neighbourhood was thick with dust in summer and unrivalled for mud in winter. Inside if you leaned even a little too much on the table it tottered, ready to fall. Its oilcloth was worn out and had holes at the four corners. The pile of straw mattresses that we spread on the floor for bedding stood on top of the old trunk. All these things in our house that were shabby, grieved me and when guests came I would leave. How could we bear to let them see us barefoot and with the old patched clothes on us? Nevertheless, I was glad they came in our door. It made me feel that we too were human beings, like the rest of the world.

When I felt the pangs of hunger, I came back home to find the divan spread with a clean, white sheet, the table with a pretty tablecloth, clean, sturdy chairs, and the pile of mattresses covered with a beautiful cloth in a leafy pattern. My mother had borrowed them from Mrs Hrístaina.

She was always helping us. Once she lent us the sailor costume belonging to her son Antónis. My mother had my photograph taken. She sent it to my godfather because of some false dream she had that he would give me financial help to study. We didn't receive a reply. To Mrs Hrístaina I owe a great debt, for the good that she did us, and more especially for the clothes she lent us for the photograph. I have it still and my childhood has not been lost from sight.

In the neighbourhood we depended on one another. One house was accustomed to borrowing things from the other, such as boiler, washtub, broom, comb, or coffee-mill. One time we had a coffee-mill too. The neighbourhood used to borrow it and that gave me great pleasure. One of the many times that we went without food for two or three days my mother sold it, together with an iron that we used to press clothes, to a the second-hand dealer just so that we could buy bread. What a torture hunger is. It takes away every happiness so that you cannot enjoy being a child.

When guests came to a house in our neighbourhood the housewife, in order to entertain them properly, would go round the doors and ask for chairs, tablecloths, plates, glasses, coffee-cups etc. They also borrowed food all the time from one another, such as an onion, a spoonful of tomato paste, a small cup of ground coffee, sugar, oil, salt or a slice of bread.

When a woman went for a visit outside the neighbourhood, she borrowed a pair of shoes, a handbag, a dress, or stockings. There were times when a woman would take off her dress and give it to another who was going on a visit. Men also borrowed among themselves shoes, clothes, or a hat. It could happen that a bridegroom would be wearing a strange suit and a bride someone else's dress.

When I returned home uncle and aunt welcomed me with delight. And their delight transferred itself to me when I saw that my new aunt was happy to be in our poor house. I felt as if they were giving me many things all at once. "Come here, you," my aunt said in a clear, sweet voice, and pulled me onto her knee. "Haven't you come to recite a little poem for us. Your uncle says you know many beautiful ones." At the same time her delicate hand caressed me on the cheek and the neck so gently that for the first time I felt the sweetness of a caress. It was unknown to me. I didn't know that anyone would need it; I thought only bread was needed. I was starved for lack of bread. I hadn't had enough of it, as with all of us. Sometimes I'm still moved remembering my first caress and the woman who taught me that such a thing existed.

When a well-dressed visitor came into our house and I saw that he was happy, I was impressed. I told this to old Zervoudákis and he replied: "It's because he sees himself as very much above you and is happy." As regards my uncle and aunt I couldn't accept this.

In winter, when the adults went off to work, Alékos and I stayed to watch over the young ones. On days when it wasn't raining we took turns to stay in, so that we could each go out. On mornings when there was frost, my brother would say to me: "So, are you going out?" Alékos was inclined to feel the cold and he was reluctant to go out first. And I was cold without clothes and my feet were stinging. The skin was cracked and they were running with blood from my being barefoot, but I was longing to go out into nature, to see the beautiful light, the mountains, the plains, the trees, the green grassy places, to hear the birds singing.

When I was near them I felt such fervour. Gradually I would become moved and my eyes would fill with tears of joy. I grew up with these sights. They made me feel better. I would forget poverty, hunger and suffering.

I would sing endlessly. I sang from the time I was young. I would fall asleep singing and wake singing; I would walk along singing. I've grown old and I still sing about this miracle that is around us.

With the spring it was time to go back to work at the furnace. One day before, I found the moulder Aléxis Skamángas. I asked him to take me on to work with him as a mould-carrier. I used to be extremely tired at that job. The pain in my shoulder was fierce. What could I do? It gave me a good wage. Moulder Aléxis didn't say that I wasn't suitable, as he did the first time. I was a year older and was more experienced. We had something else too. A common fate united us.

The first morning when we were to start work, I found them all there. We were happy. We would work and earn money to eat. I jumped for joy. When I saw them, I felt as if they were my close relatives; they had been away on a journey and had come back and we were together again. Some of them were terribly altered. They looked as if they had suddenly aged or had deliberately put on fancy costumes for a joke to act out a comedy. But if you looked at them closely, the comedy turned gradually to tragedy. With faces withered, hair turned grey, eyes sunken, and cheeks hollow, it looked as if they had suffered badly through the terrible ordeal of hunger. You knew that some of them would not be able to get through easily next time. I could see they didn't realise this and they made me pity them and feel even more sad for them.

They all greeted me with pleasure, even those who didn't pay me any attention the first year. "Welcome, little Panayótis," said one. "The good child, the singer, our hard worker," said the others.

"You have to admire him," added Nikólas, "such a young boy struggling above his strength, with a crippled shoulder, to earn his bread, like us."

This warm welcome brought tears to my eyes; that I was among such good and compassionate souls. "What's the matter? Are you crying?" asked Tzanís who was beside me. He turned and said to the others: "Hey you all, he's crying! It seems the poor lad is moved at seeing us again."

Níkos Skamángas ran over, lifted my chin with his finger and said, smiling: "The fool is really crying. His eyes are swimming in tears," and he gave me a slap on the back of the neck, instead of a hug. That was the rough way these good men expressed their love.

Some of them gathered near me. Drakoúlis lifted me up in the air. The others reached out and I found myself being carried round above their heads in their strong hands, like a little toy.

When they put me down, Nikólas said: "Let's see, are we all here?" in such a tone that it was as if he were issuing a humorous roll-call of fate. "Mathiós isn't here," said Yánnis from Pireaus.

"What's happened to him?" asked Nikólas.

"He died," replied Yánnis.

"What? He died?" many of them asked with one voice, in great surprise.

Yánnis said again more sadly: "He wasted away. Some people said it was consumption."

They were all silent, as if something had taken away their speech, and they gazed at one another as if each wanted to see in the other's face the lie we all are.

What a fairytale life is!

CRITICAL COMMENTARIES ON THE WORKS OF PANAYOTIS TRANOULIS

P. PAPANOUTSOS, Academician

In "Keratohóri" my impression is that you truly have narrative talent.

GRIGORIS KASIMATIS, Academician

My dear Mr Tranoúlis
    I thank you and congratulate you on your soul-stirring "Keratohóri".

MANOLIS ANAGNOSTAKIS, Poet

My dear Mr Tranoúlis
    My warm thanks to you for "Keratohóri". I was greatly moved when I read it.
    Sincerely yours

PAVLOS PALAIOLOGHOS, Columnist

Your "Keratohóri" enriches the literature of poverty. Your book is amazing. Thank you for this contribution.
   With my admiration

NIKIFOROS VRETTAKOS, Poet

"Keratohóri" and "For a Grape" allow us to see that Panayótis Tranoúlis is a special case. He isn't a writer who has been formed; he's a born writer.

YANNIS SKARIMBAS, Poet-Prosewriter 8-26-1972

This man (Panayótis Tranoúlis) who has written this book ("Keratohóri") is a herald of banished truth, a witness before the criminal court of humanity. He is not some unfortunate poor soul (like "The Poor Man of God," Francis of Assisi) nor is he some "blessed soul" in Christ who will inherit the Kingdom of Heaven. Who said that "guns will win"? No greater cutting edge or sharper point exists than the word-bearing sword. That is what sows and reaps Revolution. That is what proves to be the ram that gores with its horns.

   Tranoúlis reminds me of Joshua son of Nun, before Jericho with the trumpets, who made the walls tremble and the sun stand still upon Gideon and the moon in the valley of Avalon.

Please convey (to Tranoúlis of course and not . . . to Joshua Nun!) my most sincere congratulations. As for me, my insignificant self, I don't want any reparation. I seek revenge, and I bequeath to future generations the receipt for it.

NIKOLAOS LOUROS, Professor-Academician

Dear Sir:

Thank you for sending me your book, "Keratohóri". This ethnography, written with commendable simplicity and sincerity, provides proof of your literary talent which I wish you every success in developing.

NIKOLAOS LOUROS, Professor-Academician

Dear Mr Tranoúlis

Thank you for your kindness in sending me your book "From Furnace to Prison". On a previous occasion I wrote to you that you have a great talent, because you succeed not only in expressing your thoughts with simplicity but also in creating a pleasant atmosphere that holds the attention of the reader.

I cannot say that the subject you deal with interests me greatly.

But, in any case, one reads you with great pleasure.

ANDREAS TSOURAS, Poet, Journal "Thessalian Hearth" 4-3-1987

Strátis Doukas's "The Prisoner of War" has been a landmark in Greek prose. From then on many names have been admitted into this domain. Without fail, there should be added to these names the name of Panayótis Tranoúlis who, with his books "Keratohóri", "For a Grape", and "From Furnace to Prison", enters the realm of ideas as its worthy citizen. Tranoúlis penetrates into the souls of the insulted and the injured.

His word, like the aroma of warm bread and the few olives in the hand of the tired and hungry worker, asserts the respite from unhappiness that oppressed him greatly during his childhood.

He is a writer who brings alive for us an immeasurably miserable world. His relentless and rampant poverty is the source from which the unbelievable blows of life that were suffered bring discredit on the worth of human life.

The writer, standing even when his mother takes the lice from his hair with the finecomb and throws them into the brazier, does not let us be oppressed by the event but with his art sustains us by the aesthetic sensitivity of his language.

The scenes in the work of Tranoúlis have the bitter saltiness and kindling of the senses that prompt a tear from the eyes of the wounded, vulnerable, fatherless child, but we cannot fully know what this was like just by reading his books.

He has been called the Gorky of Greece, Dickens, Istráti. But nothing characterizes Panayótis Tranoúlis more than that he has given to our Modern Greek literature, with rare uniqueness, the life of a world which, without him, would have been lost.

In words of carefully chosen popular wisdom this world shines forth like a clear light from every line he writes and teaches and impresses by its simplicity.

I cannot know how Gorky's descriptions of poverty read in Russian for example, at any rate, in translation they haven't that immediacy, that "virginity" of form of Tranoúlis who perforates our doubts through and through and appears to us drenched in the "proud" tears of a life stifled by the sweat and blood of the struggle for Freedom. That's why it is not necessary to compare Panayótis Tranoúlis with the greats.

When I was reading his books, at every sentence, every tear of the writer, Poe's line "Never more, never more," hovered. His language is pure Greek to its depths. And this is Tranoúlis's gain but also ours. "Never more . . ."

HRISOTOMOS PATOULAS, Newspaper
  "Aitoloakarnaniki" August 1982

Panayótis Tranoúlis
"From Furnace to Prison"

Panayótis Tranoúlis is a special case as a writer who has dynamically and unfalteringly entered the domain of Modern Greek letters. And I say dynamically because his first book "Keratohóri" (novel 1973) took the reading public by surprise, and his second book "For a Grape" (novel 1980) proved him worthy in the minds of those who believed in him.

And they are not few.

The worthiness of a writer in the face of the yes, difficult predilections of the reading public—demands testimonies of literary elements in his works; testimonies which impress, such as clear, sound diction, personal style, and a masterly story-line suffused with lyricism. Panayótis Tranoúlis has these gifts and attributes. Certainly, in his new book "From Furnace to Prison", they unfold and spread out on every page! It is a soul-stirring account of those protagonists in his book who experienced first of all the tile-works and then prison where they were unjustly incarcerated.

The pictures in the book unfold with a naturalness which captivates because you feel that you are experiencing alongside you, the sighs of his heroes. Here we can see the writing talent of Panayótis Tranoúlis.

In a simple and completely personal style, using sound and effortless language, and with a strong and genuine story-line, enriched by humanity and true feelings, he unfolds scenes from life with simplicity and sincerity and makes them into a living art—an art whose target and purpose is to make us think but also to stir our soul. He writes on page 29: ". . . We suffered a lot from the food we were given. We went through most days eating dry food. Only on Sundays did we eat a hot meal. We washed ourselves, shaved off the week's beard, and washed our clothes. Sometimes we would make a crude patch for our clothes." How truly sensitive he is and with what expressive density he externalizes his thoughts! And on page 147, he writes: ". . . *You* ask me if I suffer. I would like *him* to ask me, even if he hurt me two or three times or more. Their indifference to human suffering wounds you. And to think that they speak the same language, that they are our people. They're Greeks, our brothers of the same blood." How much humanity is hidden in these words! Words that reach the heart and leave a mark behind! Panayótis Tranoúlis has persuaded us. He is a born writer.

Hrisóstomos Patoúlas

NIKOS SPANIAS, Poet, Newspaper "National Herald" New York 8-29-1980 (about "Keratohóri")

Heart-rending. Only with this word can I describe the stories that make up the chronicle of life in a village, of a poor neighbourhood, written by the prosewriter Panayótis Tranoúlis. Yes, heart-rending and not in a few places, soul-stirring. "It is hard to write down all I saw and lived through. There are many things I cannot bear to tell. I write the things that leave me heart to breathe." The writer puts these words down as a title page to his book which is so engaging, so expert and so appealing "the things that leave me heart to breathe." Indeed. But sometimes the narrative has such vividness and energy that it takes one's breath away.

In an enlightening forward to "Keratohóri" Vasílis Rótas and Voúla Damianákou write that "it is the yardstick which measures the gap of social injustice and inequality. Very few such images of life have been given us. Here people are not play-acting, they are not telling sad stories in order to be pitied, in order to persuade our philanthropic society that they are chocking . . ." Exactly. If, as Rótas and Damianákou write, in "Keratohóri" there are no adornments, no figures of speech it is because poverty itself—callous and implacable— strangles the outcasts of fate, the poor unfortunates, the wrecks of life.

I read—or rather devoured—the 140 pages of the book before I realized that nowhere had I seen the writer raving although he is stunned with pain, although the misery and poverty hour by hour threaten to drag him, like a small, broken twig, into the muddy gutter. What mud, what mud-covered people pass through these pages.

Mud-covered literally, and most of them sullied by poverty and lack of work. The cycle of their utterly wretched life begins in the summer at a furnace where bricks are made, is interrupted during the icy winter (when the mud and rain pour into their houses) and continues the following summer. Half the time exhaustion, the other half exasperation. Occasionally, in the middle of the exhausting work, they ask a worker where so and so is. "He died," someone replies, and the workers continue with their work . . . If wealth corrupts, so much more does poverty. Without vapid sermonizing, false romanticism, empty rhetorical figures of speech, Panayótis Tranoúlis, describing life in its almost indescribable misery, presents us with characters so vivid that they seem carved in relief. The narrator, or better still, annotator is a child, Panayótis Tranoúlis at a tender age—who sees everything around him with innocence and yet with wisdom: "Immediately after my father's death, my mother took me and my brother, Alékos to work in the brick furnace belonging to Pandelís Krápas. Here, our father had worn out what was left of the strength in his hands." This is the unaffected and heart-rending opening sentence in "Keratohóri". The significant statement: "Here our father had worn out what was left of the strength in his hands", says it all. This short sentence has the power of an overture to an opera, or a symphony, the symphony of toiling humanity, of inhuman ill-treatment, of beggary, of shameless mendicity, of hunger, of the wan smile.

The pages of Panayótis Tranoúlis reminded me of the pages of Dickens, Gorky (his famous autobiography, "In Strange Hands"), of Panaït Istráti ("Mrs Kyralína"). I'm saying they *reminded* me only—because there you meet—enough to take your breath away—the herd of the destitute and the hell of the persecuted. But I'm saying, and I emphasize, that Panayótis Tranoúlis in forceful and expressive language writes his very own, original symphony of human bondage. "The moulders," he writes, "had neardivine power over us." Do not pass lightly over the word "neardivine", it is Panayótis Tranoúlis's word (among many others equally successful) and they have their own stature, their own breath, their own colour, their own radiance . . . for example: "Our homes were near the furnace and when any of us apprentices, children seven to twelve years old, was being given a thrashing he could be heard in the whole neighbourhood. From the cries of each of us our mothers knew which one they were beating. Occasionally somebody's mother would arrive in tears. She would wipe the blood from his face and whisper to him: 'Why don't you do what you're told child? What did you do to make him butcher you like this? Watch out or he'll kill you sometime.' " The ugly face of poverty. Terrible. Heart-rending. The life of a poor man is a continuous humiliation with the dregs of bitterness and self-knowledge. Talking about the boss, the moulder Aléxis Skamángas (who was an artist at his work) says: "What does he want, interfering with us? Isn't the job done? Do we beat the children, or does he? *He* beats them with our hands. As if we're not sorry for them? I look at them and pity them from my heart but what can I do about it? I beat them unwillingly. We drive them hard. From the morning we push them to the limits; we work them to death. They're young children. They get tired, and we thrash them on top of that. We steal their childhood from them for a day's pay. But look how the boss demands ten thousand bricks a day from each bench. In other furnaces they produce only nine. Who beats the children then? We or the boss?" Rótas and Damianákou sum up this book as a series of tragic peaks (the son beats his mother, the thugs knife each other for drugs and through sheer bravado, the young children are burned by the hot bricks). There is great suffering, but nowhere are there bewailings, superfluous words or histrionics. On the contrary, there is understanding, high principles, forgiveness, courage, and even humour which is also one of the marks of true poetry . . ."

Panayótis (he refers only once to his name throughout the book and his surname once, in the diminutive Tranoulákis) barefoot winter and summer, is thrown roughly out by the watchdogs of the church. "You must wear shoes to come in here," they ordered. One time he puts on a pair of new tan shoes (a gift from an uncle) and dares to go into church.

The watchdogs hiss at him to get out, and Panayótis, calmly, as if he were saying his prayers, bends down and whispers into the ear of one of them: "I'm wearing shoes . . ."

How moving! How very moving. A book that deserves to be read by all of us.

GRIGORIS YERASIMOS, Short story writer, Journal
  "Aeolian Letters" 2-1-1973

A child who begins the struggle to earn a living at the age of seven years without ever going to school, who has a premature taste of a life with the cruelty and heartlessness of those around him (also tormented themselves by poverty and misfortune), is not by any means an uncommon phenomenon, even today in an affluent society.

And yet that this child, growing up far from God, in the midst of daily insatiable greed, in a poor neighbourhood among poor and illiterate people, should manage to succeed professionally, to find his feet through his ingeniousness and become a creative element in the narrow circle of the market square in Keratohóri—his shanty town—and this is not something unprecedented. However the fact that this young person managed to preserve his humanity and fulfil his dream (who knows what strength had been grafted on to his young soul from an early age), that he was able to develop his mind and educate himself in conditions in which those of the same age were left stranded in the swamp of that "debased life" or sank into vagrancy and crime—this is the strange and rare phenomenon. And the fruit of this service to life and to intellect is "Keratohóri", a narrative-novel by Mr Tranoúlis, a book in which a world comes to life, the world of tough struggle, the world of the slum-dwellers and down-trodden; the struggle for bread and pride comes to life. Here cruelty alternates with sensitivity and brutish indifference with brave moments of elation. And everything is written and expressed in a frank, direct language, without pointless convolutions, without posing and clamouring but rather is written in a low voice, the voice of calm truth, sometimes with bitterness, sometimes with tenderness and always with purity of heart that guides his hand to write. The writer is a genuine "primitive", perhaps more genuine that Nik. Nikolaïdis, the Cypriot and Strátis Doúkas who first opened up this kind of writing in Modern Greek narrative. Tranoúlis, the writer of "Keratohóri" belongs—by analogy—to this school in which Maxim Gorky and Istráti are classed among those writers who stooped to the lowest dregs of lower-class life and didn't simply observe it but lived it fully.

DIMITRIS FOTIADIS, Historian and playwright
7-21-1975

Mr Panayótis Tranoúlis
    Our mutual and dear friend Vasílis Rótas gave me your "Keratohóri". I've read it now that I'm on holiday in a little house that I have here in Néo Voutzá.
    What hell and what humanity!

Many episodes were soul-stirring as they presented themselves in a text that life itself has imprinted.. It could be a novel.

But fortunately for the reader it is reality, as you had the sad privilege of living it in your harsh childhood years. For this reason your offering takes on the greatness of an unrepeatable experience.

DIMITRIS FOTIADIS, Historian and playwright
11-4-1980

Dear Panayótis Tranoúlis
Thank you for your book "For a Grape". It has the virtue of simplicity in its form and of richness in experience of life.
Sincerely yours

NIKOS GALAZIS, Poet-Prosewriter, Journal "New Thinking" 10-8-1977

You have only to read the first line and you won't put the book down—until the last line. The writer's testimony is vivid and animated. It is a record of a certain time, making up an anatomy of composite incidents and is expressed laconically.

In the book one can discern an abyss of feelings and experiences. It is an inexhaustible and fearful goldmine or diamond mine from which you break away with the axe of your emotional response rough pieces that glow and dazzle your soul with their greatness.

I took notice of the fact that the writing in "Keratohóri" exhales hope and love of life, joyful contemplation, and reflective confrontation with life.

The goodness, the infinite humanity, endurance, honesty and high principle. In his unbearable hunger there is no-one to stretch a hand out to another's possession so that he could appropriate even a crumb or a bitter orange. From a dreadful and horrible fate only the soul emerges intact, impervious, and incorruptible. The supreme conscience. Prideful and inherent nobleness.

From out of the pages of P. Tranoúlis, from beginning to end, one hears the whisper of a sublime music. From out of the words, the phrases, the magical scenes, a distinctive song, the beauty of popular tradition materializes. "I would sing endlessly. I sang from the time I was very young and became aware of myself. I grew up with song. I would wake singing; I would walk along the street singing. I've grown old and I still sing about this miracle that is around us."

Life itself. People barefoot in the harsh winter, emotion blurred with tears from the blows of fate and nature, the prey of others in a pitiless society. Struggle with the dead and the shipwrecked—a world where people died like flies.

This book of P. Tranoúlis set me thinking, because it was written by a man who didn't set foot in a school and the little that he knew he learned himself when he was already an adult, reading with difficulty the newspapers or other printed material that fell into his hands. However, he studied in the

University of Life. He went through examinations and excelled and this book is his doctoral thesis.

An autobiographical book written with so much truth, as much truth as those who struggle honestly with life can bear, written with ingenuousness, without exaggeration and from rich experience, is worthy of a place among the masterpieces of our more recent literature that are representative and worthy hallmarks of its progress. "Keratohóri" is a book in this category that has nothing like it in our literature. The life of the writer has analogies with the life of Gorky and Panaït Istráti. Gorky was also left an orphan at the age of four. He struggled to survive and became a vagrant. He kept inside him an adventurous spirit, as did Istráti. Our writer was thrown mercilessly into the struggle to survive a dog's life, to record honestly the potential of an abominable cannibalistic machine.

His pages are in the universal spectrum and will illumine the literature of every developed country, pages that a Gorky would sign unhesitatingly.

IASON EVANGELOU, Poet-Prosewriter, Journal "New Thinking" 9-8-1973

Panayótis Tranoúlis's book "Keratohóri" is a story in the form of a novel but in essence a personal experience which is transubstantiated in artistic language. With effortless sincerity and pure lyricism—where it is necessary—the writer tells us about human misfortune, suffering and poverty, the exhausting work, hunger and illness, humiliation and mockery, despair and treachery. And all this, without being given to lamentation, but with honesty and bravery he doesn't cease to point out and emphasize humanity and love, wherever he finds it, and also hope and faith in man.

With unaffected artistry he writes the history of his epoch objectively and uncovers the social body.

The frugal expression combined with expressive density, the sensitivity and his narrative gift, as well as the power of his reflections, win us over.

NIKOS ZERVAKIS, Writer 12-19-1990

Pure people like Mr Panayótis Tranoúlis are like distant meteorites which have the immutable elements of original creation, and only occasionally visit the surface of our troubled world to give a simple and luminous message to the generations of today and tomorrow—that we started off simple and pure and we should remain like this, he proclaims.

YANNIS KORIDIS, Prosewriter, Journal "Iolkós"

For the first time I have come into contact with the prose works of Panayótis Tranoúlis. I feel guilty. I hadn't happened to have read his earlier book "Keratohóri" (1973). Reading "For a Grape" was the motive, and I got through "Keratohóri" in one go as well. It was right that this should have happened because I would have a complete picture of Tranoúlis's work. Blessed be the moment it happened. I thank my good friend who sent it to me.

Panayótis Tranoúlis with his new book "For a Grape" reveals the many capabilities of his talent. His language flows effortlessly. Blunt and penetrating it not only touches but jolts the reader to a point which happens only with writers in the ranks of Maxim Gorky, Panaït Istráti, and Menélaos Loudémis. Experiences which start from his earliest childhood years filled with bitterness, orphanhood and abject poverty. Realistic and talented, consistent and precise in creating his template he revives an entire life, a life exceptional for its subsequent development. The young, fatherless child shoulders all the consequences of responsibility for the daily bread. Life began for him in a hut in Peristéri with his mother and sisters. Difficult and harsh years for an unprotected family. They had to be so careful about everything, hence the scrimping and saving, the privations and sacrifices so as to be able to stay alive. One brother was away from home. The mother had given him to a stock-farmer to look after the sheep just for his food. Tranoúlis tells us how his mother used to say: "He's not strong. He won't last at it. He'll die of hunger." We immediately understand what gears he will have to engage. He first encounters in the furnace of the Sacred Way the iron vise of society that will squeeze his weak little hands.

Tranoúlis, with particular mastery, creates his own atmosphere. The language comes over clear, and sets up vividly the scene of the action. The neighbourhood with its own problems, the people of the neighbourhood with their own personal histories, their everyday worries convey a distinctive atmosphere throughout the writer's work. But the children, those poor children who have dreams, like all children in all social classes, are the writer's yeast. Tragic moments. Thomás, the lad with the accordion will die for a grape; an unscrupulous guard will kill him. As we close the last page the first page continues to dominate.

Before us, we have a born writer, a craftsman of language. I shall repeat what Vasílis Rótas and Voúla Damianákou noted in the prologue to "Keratohóri": "The scenes he describes are so vivid and have such immediacy that the reader's participation in them becomes so intense and all-embracing it creates in him the feeling that he himself, without any intermediary, is living this nightmare life."

YANNIS MOUGHOPANNIS, Journalist, Newspaper "Thessaly" 5-20-1973

By right and with spirit Panayótis Tranoúlis enters the literary arena.

"Keratohóri" is the book that speaks to the heart of each of us, that raises questions, a book in which the glance becomes a scalpel and the thought a fire. The writer, a child of poverty, fatherless and with a heavy burden on his shoulders lifted his cross and stood upright. He didn't give in; he didn't lose heart; he didn't sell his dreams, nor was he lost in confusion in the thousand and one alleys of the easy life. He struggled alone with fate and with people; he stood up straight against obstacles; he overcame the stumbling-blocks that were flung in his path, and arrived victorious on the bright road of life. Struggle and responsibility to the finishing line that has been crowned with the olive branch of victory. The experiences he acquired, most of the time inhuman and disheartening, didn't prove capable of diverting the road mapped out. On the contrary they reinforced his will and urged him onward all the stronger.

The chronicle of fatherlessness, poverty, and struggle make up the pages of this book which is also a ballad of struggling humanity.

There are neither compromises with conscience nor turnings left or right away from the road mapped out, only striving and victories. The book expresses with immediacy and realism the life of every person who strives to stand on his own feet and prosper. The dry land of deliverance awaits him to crown him the victor. It is enough not to betray his own life. This is the message that justifies the attempt of the new man of letters, and that promises new flights with the free, unbound wings of memory.

SOPHIA MAVROEIDI-PAPADAKI, POET 4-23-1972

Dear Mr Tranoúlis

After a very painful family experience, "Keratohóri" came into my hands. I devoured it so to speak, as I have had similar experiences—in other ways—of the struggle to earn a living in childhood. How much animation, how much truth, what humanity are within these very fine pages of yours. And how simply and vividly you present life to us. The people, the characters, the events are portrayed with blood and tears, and so simply, as from the heart. And beyond question, the talent of the poet, the narrator, the creator shines through.

The description to the smallest detail, so tender with humane feeling, is a source of joy, and a slap in the face for society. You've made a bright start in your creative work. We expect a lot more from you because suffering has taught you, without drying up the freshness of your heart.

The Rótas-Damianákou introduction is marvellous.

SOPHIA MAVROEIDI-PAPADAKI 11-27-1987

Dear Mr Tranoúlis

I read with love your book "For a Grape". You are an amazing writer and I admire you for your humanity, your sensitivity, and your power of observation. You are made of the same stuff as Gorky and Istráti and you see things in the world with the same eye. You manage to make a detail into an art that pleases. You manage to make the insignificant take on the dimensions of the great. With your language rich in feeling you are able to present life as it flows. You have the gift from on high. Please accept my warm congratulations and my love.

DINOS BLAHOYANNIS, Journal "New Thinking"
2-6-1976

There are clashing rocks[1] in our memory that close when we approach and try to pass through them. There are moments that make our hearts bleed and trap our thoughts in the pain that we have gone through. That's why we turn away from, or moderate or justify unhappy repressed childhood experiences as the doctors would say, who, in psychoanalysing us, would make out that we are ill.

An exception is the "Hunger" of Knut Hamsun who forgot it in the Great War because he was well-fed and Panaït Istráti and Kazanóvas who talked as openly as it was possible for them to do.

I would say that Maxim Gorky was projecting a sure and broader picture of the world. He proved that privation operates without anger in the struggle to create a work.

But there is a difference that weighs heavily in the work of Panayótis Tranoúlis, namely the absence of any attempt at embellishment of the narrative which would work to inhibit the participation of the reader and the emotion which pours from his raw, realistic language of the people.

In the works of those writers I have referred to above, there appears the literary lining which indeed adds to the depiction of low life. May I be permitted to say that the insertion of scenes in the form of works of art to describe physi-

---

[1]The clashing rocks—*symplighádes*—in Homer's Odyssey were supposed to close on all who sailed between them.

cal space, the sea, the forest, the sky draws you far away from participation and makes you merely an observer of a tragic and unjust society.

Here you sink with Panayótis Tranoúlis up to the neck in mud and you yourself are drowning. You see that there are people who do not die from great poverty but their spirit is broken. They die from their great misfortune because they haven't the money to bury their dead.

In "Keratohóri" I recognise the nobleness of phrase of Skambitséfski who, commenting on the work of Nikolai Gogol, writes that "it is truly marvellous that you compel the reader to finish the book with a sad feeling and to cry out together with the hero: "This world is tedious, gentlemen!"

Here you close the book and you are amazed, because you are confronted with a boundless goodness, so far-reaching that the beatings, the nakedness, the hunger, the disaster, the pain, the brutality, the absence of care do not engender a trace of hatred in the purity of his heart. Thus the tediousness is so polite, so smooth that with difficulty you hold yourself back from it to cry out alone under the weight of the heavy "strike" that cripples the tender shoulder of the lymphatic child: "This world is evil, you wretched souls!"

It should be noted that my dear friends, the couple, Vasílis Rótas and Voúla Damianákou, who have produced a lasting work[2] so sound and in accordance with the progressive spirit of the time, uncompromising and unyielding they

---

[2]This refers to their great translation of the work of Shakespeare.

have played a role in the case of Panayótis Tranoúlis like that of Romain Rolland who discovered Panaït Istráti. If I may be allowed my humble opinion "this book with its tragic peaks", as the writers of the preface note, needs to be continued.

The writer notes that it is difficult to write about everything he saw and lived through. There are many things he cannot bear to write about. He writes only about those things that leave him the heart to breathe. But I believe, and this is apparent from his book, that he has boundless strength and goodness in that he can remember, forgive, and record the inhuman ways of a society where the slave by tradition becomes the torturer of his little fellow-worker so that they should both support on their ravaged backs a rotten and vile structure. I confess that I haven't read any other book with such sad stories and such tragic scenes of a life of martyrdom. I recall a family of twelve in Vóha who died of tuberculosis one after the other. They were carried on the wooden bedstead to be prayed over and buried. In the café the villagers would cross themselves, shake their heads and say: "What can you do about them? Who's to feed them?"

And a thick-skinned landowner would always add: "And the one who's died—why the devil did he want so many children!"

But this calamity that appears so plainly before us is an unknown corner whose existence you wouldn't even have suspected.

For that reason you're sorry you're no longer young enough to start the struggle again with clenched teeth.

MARIA MANDOUVALOU 7-11-2001

Mr Tranoúlis

I confess that at first I confronted your work with mistrust, for many reasons. When I read your books—which I confess I didn't know about—although I should have—I felt—chiefly with "My Life in the Furnace"—that I was in fact dealing with an autodidact, a self-educated person with a very significant talent and not heard of through circles and various cliques.

I shall teach you to our students.

Sincerely

M. Mandouválou

STELIOS GHERANIS, Poet 6-24-1982

My dear Tranoúlis

"For a Grape" is not a book like those that any scribbler reels off for us. It is a warm human body; blood and tears flow from it. But the important thing is that the two of them, the blood and the tears reach your reader filtered and clear. They have passed through the purgatory of your conscience and have been enriched with light. The bitter and bloody struggle of your heroes takes on beneficial dimensions for us. You transmit to us, in the harsh times in which we live, human nobleness and goodness, the first steps in narrative, that bring to mind great moments in world literature. You have written soul-stirring pages in which the language flows effortlessly from a rich inner source. You confirm and strengthen the impression that "Keratohóri" evoked in me. You are a powerful and vivid prose writer with admirable narrative mastery. I shake your hand with love.

YORGHIS HALATSAS, Short story writer

Dear Panayótis

Your book "From Furnace to Prison" has taken a place in my library. This is a prose work that I read with great attention and it moved me. Moreover, this is not just my discovery. Its republication in the fourth edition alone says it all. It clearly demonstrates the love of the general reader for a book that deserves it. The narrative, which is characterized by little nuances the interchange of characters, events, and incidents, creates a crowning contribution which does you honour. The whole structure of the book proceeds from the need to present with clarity experiences that carry the seed in them to become art and to last in time. I believe the book leaves a sincere and deep emotion in each person who reads it. I thank you.

Yórghis Halatsás

ILIAS SIMOPOULOS, Poet 12-29-1973

Dear Mr Tranoúlis
Thank you for "Keratohóri". Your simple, substantial, precise language reveals a writer endowed with a great talent. It is a notable contribution to our prose. I wish you a creative and happy 1974.

ILIAS SIMOPOULOS, Poet 12-12-1980

Dear Mr Tranoúlis
I thank you for your kindness in sending me your book "For a Grape". I have always discerned your talent for prose writing. Now my faith has been consolidated. You are a born prose writer. I wish you happy holidays and a creative new year.

ILIAS SIMOPOULOS, Poet 3-24-1982

Dear Mr Tranoúlis
Your new book "From Furnace to Prison" is as spontaneous, truthful, and revealing, as are all your works. It holds the avid interest of the reader. It stirs the soul; it enlightens; it teaches.
With my greetings
Ilías Simópoulos

YORGHOS VALETAS, Journal "Aeolian Letters"
8-8-1981

When an excellent prose work was published five years ago
under the title "Keratohóri" and was praised unreservedly
and unanimously by the critics, Panayótis Tranoúlis, previ-
ously unknown in the literary world, showed that he possessed a genuine literary talent. With a narrative style that
doesn't depart from popular speech and has all its gifts—naturalness, simplicity, vividness, brevity, and charm. Well then,
after this unique book in which some critics found analogies
with Gorky, Panaït Istráti and Hamsun, Panayótis Tranoúlis
has given us his second book which essentially complements
the first one, in form as well as in content. The title of the new
prose work is "For a Grape" which describes the childhood
of the writer with its misery and the suffocating atmosphere,
a childhood in which the various grim events left an indelible
scar on his soul and the recollection and recording of which
enriches his narrative with humanity and true feeling. It is the
chronicle of the life of a village boy who never knew joy in
his life, but was brought up in poverty and tasted the bitterness of the harsh struggle to survive. Panayótis Tranoúlis's
new book begins with the move from his house in Peristéri to
the German huts outside the detached houses where his
mother managed to get refugee accommodation. With rare
vividness he describes the features of his mother, his uncles,
his sisters, the foremen and, in particular, his boss from
whom he brought away memories of the harshest experiences
that wounded his young soul, to the point where even today,

the writer's suffering overflows from the narrative like a groan or a cry of pain.

This book of childhood memories is full of humane feeling because he reveals and justifies the human suffering of the working class, in the poor neighbourhood, in the rubbish dump where, for a grape, a thoughtless child loses his life.

This chapter, as well as the following one, "He passed me by without speaking" as well as some others, like "Lalaoúnis and his bench", "The feast-day", "My job with Nikákias", are some of the most polished in the book. Without the other chapters being inferior so that they would show some changes and differences in quality.

This originates from the fact that Panayótis Tranoúlis speaks from the heart and writes, as some critics from the past have said, "with his blood," without any affectation.

Let's look at the first part of the chapter "For a Grape": "Above the rubbish dump there was an endless plain of vineyards. The child was beguiled and stretched out his hand. The guard, whose hut was a little further away, saw him, fired at him and killed him. This man was very tall with dark, almost black skin. He had a big moustache. When you saw him your heart was in your mouth. He always went about with the gun on his back and would say boastingly: 'Whoever dares reach out to cut a grape in the vineyard will die on the spot!' There was a road running through the vineyards and whenever any of us happened to be passing through there we would look only straight ahead. We were afraid to look right or left. When we looked the guard assumed we wanted to cut some grapes and he had shot many people . . .

. . . When he saw Thomás was killed, his eyes widened. They became red like a fierce fire and he shouted in a terrible rage: 'Where's he gone?'

'He went that way,' replied Mastrolouloúdas, as pale as a sheet, and raised his hand slowly towards where the murderer had fled.

'There he is!' said the teacher stretching out his short arm. We all looked where he was pointing.

The guard was just visible. The length of the plain had swallowed his huge height. He looked like a tiny little thing. When you saw him you couldn't believe that this insignificant thing was able to do something so evil. We all ran after the guard, we young ones following close behind. Pandelís Vláhos was running out in front. The fields had filled with people. The distance which separated us from the murderer was shortening and he became more and more visible. In one hand he held the rifle and on his other shoulder he had thrown his jacket. With his gigantic height he looked fearsome. As they came near him they threw stones at him. Pandelís shouted fiercely at him: 'Give yourself up, murderer! Wherever you go you won't escape. You'll die!'

On hearing this I was frightened. The guard turned the barrel of his rifle and shot at us. The terrifying sound spread over the plain. We scattered, running into ditches, behind olive trees and willows, wherever each of us could go. As the guard was running away the whole crowd went behind him with stones, their raging voices resounding over the plain. 'Murderer, you won't escape. You'll pay with your life for what you did!' . . ."

In this clear, effortless and unaffected style that revives popular oral speech in its genuine form, Panayótis Tranoúlis's whole book is written. It confirms the impression given by his first book and assures him an eminent place as a demotic prosewriter in Greek literature, another Doúkas.

VANGELIS NIKOLOUDIS, Editor-in-Chief, Journal "Bibliographical Review" October 1996

Dear friend

I have reread your book "My Life in the Furnace".

Oscar Wilde affirmed that "the book that isn't worth reading twice isn't worth reading at all". My conclusion is that "My Life in the Furnace" is full of vividness and humanity. The experiences are constructed with technical mastery and with the pure material of a personal style.

If Maxim Gorky had not preceded you in time, I would have dared to call you his teacher.

In the structure of the book the careful reader discovers four qualities of fundamental importance in life that encourage high-mindedness and enterprising success. It concerns firstly the innate optimism with the eyes of which one can see opportunities even in difficulties (Winston Churchill), secondly love of learning which bestows a deeper knowledge of the wisdom of men (Maxim Gorky), thirdly the exemplary honesty that is elevated to duty (Dumas), and finally constant labour that is embraced religiously (Paul the Apostle).

From the very beginning and as I continue reading the

book I feel within me the expansion of your contribution, transformed into brightly coloured pictures of experienced truth, truth which cruelly and pitilessly scourged the tender soul of the child and which on his "butchered", innocent face the cruel and pitiless punisher, arrogantly abuses and spits on society.

And so, my friend, breaking through the surface with the power of your mind and cutting away all restraints with your lancet, sharpened on the whetstone of your free soul, you enter unfalteringly into the deepest interior of life. And the reader goes onwards with you, drawing lessons continuously from you.

It is this last quality that gives even more value to your presence among writers.

STRATIS ANASTASELLIS, Prosewriter 10-17-1978

Dear friend

I've been two days in Yohánesbourg—Ioannoúpolis according to the purists who mistreated Shakespeare by changing his name to "Sekspíros", who decline Míler as "Míleros". Amsterdam becomes "Amsterlódamo"—and may the devil take them.

The only intellectual companion I brought with me is your "Keratohóri" which I read, study, and can't get enough of. I shed tears with Panayotákis, sigh and admire the man (if you can call the child a man) who is buffeted by his fate, the fate of the world. Today the 17th of the month I encountered . . .

. . . Keep well my friend. I read your "Keratohóri" and your heroes, the furnace workers struggle along here too with different coloured skin, collecting blows on the head from their civilised bosses who teach them how to bow their heads. But I saw that in bowing they justified themselves and were contemplating their freedom. I've gone on too long about this but I wanted to vent my anger. Give our best wishes to your good lady. Many greetings from myself and my wife.

VALAVANIS KYRIAKOS, Prosewriter Critic

From his book "Critical Studies" on the work of Panayótis Tranoúlis

(Important essay conveying a most sharp critical thinking and substantiated opinion on the incalculable contribution of the writer. Extract from this book:)

A work of concentration of thought which brings honor to the field of Greek literature. I think he should take his place as the Theóphilos[3] of Literature. And let's say too that if other nations have a Gorky, an Istráti, a Hamsun or a Dickens we have a Panayótis Tranoúlis.

---

[3]Theóphilos—Yórghos Hatzimihaíl, significant representative of Greek popular painting (1866-1934).

LILI MAVROKEFALOU, Writer

Mr Tranoúlis

With your warm, mature, unadorned writing you uniquely bring to life the pitiless world of your youth, simultaneously lighting it up with hope, goodness, and faith. Your genuine literary talent serves truth, denounces social injustice, and inspires. The reader effortlessly participates in the events narrated, identifies with the people, is imbued by your passion for life, drawing courage and principles from that source.

In our very much easier, yet in other ways, difficult and confused times we need your books, our young people most of all. I thank you for the pleasure your stories have given me, the pleasure that contact with true art gives. It has been a long time since I felt it.

Líli Mavrokefálou

HRISTOS LEVANTAS, Short story writer

Excellent friend

I received your book "Keratohóri" and I thank you most warmly, not only for your noble offering, but also for the great pleasure you have given me. Without question this is a text that enriches with its frugal expressiveness and most profound humanity, its dynamic prose with its abundant, realistic colours, and its immediacy; it brings honour to our modern prose writing.

I shall write on the subject when I am able but I should have loved the opportunity of ringing the bells to proclaim the value of your contribution.

Sincere congratulations

NIKI GARIDI, Poet-Prosewriter 12-13-1989

Dear Mr Tranoúlis

Spangler says "Whoever has written about his country and his era has written about all countries and all eras."

And that is what Panayótis Tranoúlis has achieved in giving our literature this wonderful book "My Life in the Furnace". He has recorded an epoch which would have been lost if it hadn't been described by this seven year old child who was seared by poverty, toil, and suffering.

I didn't know whom to thank. First of all God who left me, so be it, with a little light, to savour this soul-stirring book, or my childhood friend, Mítsos Kanellópoulos or the author Panayótis Tranoúlis who shattered and scorched me.

I shall confine myself to a THANK YOU and a bow of homage to the Gift of God which He literally bestowed upon the seven year old boy who became the creator of this soul-stirring book.

I am not a critic to be able to convey the depth of the book. But I can say that the pages of the book shocked me. I would say it is a Gospel that teachers should read on the first day of every week to their class in school so that they and their pupils learn about the times when other children of toil,

MY LIFE IN THE FURNACE

hunger, and dignity lived. Children who loved and felt sorry for their parents and their brothers and sisters, who shared their bite of food with the hungry, their strength with the helpless, who held out a hand to the unfortunate, who respected the people they worked under and knew and could distinguish between the honest person and the Judas. They could learn too that some other children didn't know anything about carefree play; they never had enough bread to eat and they were mature from the age of seven. Such books ought to be among the first to be taught in schools and universities. But now they throw the children into affluence and create thieves and murderers.

We were hungry then but didn't touch what didn't belong to us. We worked from when we were children to help the ailing mother, the younger brothers and sisters. We went to school and when we got out we would hurry off to the fields to help.

We loved work and our fellow human-beings. We felt sorry for one another. We would weep when we had a grievance about something and joke immediately after. We laughed in order to forget what was wounding us at the time.

Dear brother, Mr Tranoúlis, thank you for this emotion that your writing has inspired in me. The description of life in the furnace goes like a lancet close to the bone. Page 76 of the book is outstanding. Christ had nothing of his own. He taught love and everything held in common, a world without boundaries and wealth shared out.

How humane you are. What far-reaching speculations you present: "The weakness of a young child was the strength

~ 173 ~

that protected them". What philosophy and development of thought in this sentence.

But what page should I refer to first? All of them bleed, all of them hurt, such as pages 107, 108, 109, 110, tragic pages with excellent psychography of scene. The child crying for fear his mother should die and the sensitive heart of old Apostólis; on page 111 a knife in my heart because my father too died young a broken man because of a friend who had cheated on him. Yes and I too as a small child tasted the bitterness of being orphaned and poor. Those pages are so much mine that your own blessed hands have written so vividly! This crafted narrative language of yours with the beautiful, tragic scenes of the life of the people at that time, scenes that continue still for certain people, goes straight to the heart and circulates in the blood of the reader. The description of an era like which I haven't lived, those pages 123-124 and 125-126, such life-like pictures, written with realism, stir the soul. The psychology and psychography, the bitterness and grief of the children, the tribulations of the mother are powerful, incomparable pages which only a remarkable creator could produce. In each page one can comprehend an entire world and stand among the people in it. This exhaustive description of people, so superbly produced, all the situations, all the individuals, all those moments of daily routine that mark an epoch—a lancet that goes close to the bone.

The poverty, that tragically proud poverty, that made hearts bleed and strengthened such an honourable, and beautiful character—one can't bear this grief in the heart and one wonders are there such writers of such talents who should be considered among the first rank, and few know about them because their circumstances didn't help them.

I grieved, I wept, completely shattered by this book of frugal expression, sensation, power of observation, vivid language, and the life of a world where people had to strive hard for a mouthful of bread and a bit of self-respect.

Sculptor of the soul of the tormented in the furnace, in simple writing and with penetrating gaze he has exceeded the limits of the reader's endurance.

I read the book without pause in one night. I would say that I "received" it as I would Holy Communion. It stirred me to the depths. I took it to my heart and I kept it beside me with pages marked so that I can open the book at difficult moments and drink from memory and find my courage when I lose it.

I end with gratitude to its creator and the wish that he stay strong and courageous and give us other masterpieces, and my thanks to God and Mítsos Kanellópoulos who introduced me to this work.

With much esteem

YORGHOS POLITARHIS, Writer

It must have taken much thought on the part of Panayótis Tranoúlis to write about life in a world full of goodness and anguish. His book is a chronicle of the life of brick and tile furnace workers but it takes on the breadth of a literary work since its writer is equipped with sensitivity and power of observation.

He stood beside the poor. He saw their faults and virtues and emphasised whatever good exists in the human soul. Because of this his language comes to us warm and instantly alive. You would think they were pages of a diary written at the time of the events. You do not tire of reading this book; on the contrary you delight in it. His characters are real people imbued with the light of spiritual glimmerings. They become familiar, as if we had known them for a long time. And the dialogue, wherever it occurs, is very dramatic. He doesn't adorn his style with loquacity and literary devices, features of our modern literature. With measured simplicity he portrays the social environment, as did our earlier writers who were the teachers of this type of writing. Mr Tranoúlis comes as representative of the working-class narrative and will be thus classified in the future, and thus he is regarded in their preface by our teachers Vasílis Rótas and Voúla Damianákou.. Vasílis Rótas is not being partial, he is not mistaken, and for that reason Mr Tranoúlis should rest assured of his talent.

YANNIS MARRES, Poet-Prosewriter 3-5-1973

Dear Mr Tranoúlis

I thank you with all my heart for the great emotion I felt reading your marvellous book!

Since, on the one hand my dear, good friends in their prologue, and on the other hand you in your text, have covered everything, what can one say. Nothing!

There's no need for me to say anything more. Only that I feel like giving thanks for the life that tormented you, seared you, literally wounded you and gave you to us as something marvellous, complete, full of strength and humanity, to shake us to the depths with things that rouse emotion, something which so rarely visits us in these confused times.

I warmly shake your hand.

YANNIS MARRES 3-14-1981

(About the book "For a Grape")
My dear Panayótis

I thank you with all my heart for your, in many respects, distinguished book, which you had the kindness to send me. You moved me deeply with all the things you write in your book, things that are related to your life and your sufferings, things that, written by you in such a simple and beautiful way, not only move their reader deeply but also compel him to think about many things in life or man's life and work . . .

Stay well and write and keep sending me your books.

DENIS TZANNATOS, Newspaper 11-22-2002

Panayótis Tranoúlis: The selfless lover of letters

The fact is that he could inspire the theme for the making of a film for the cinema or even a television series.

Moreover he himself has recorded the scenario of his life

in the four autobiographical books that he has published so far.

For this reason Panayótis Tranoúlis represents a special case for Greek letters.

From childhood he knew the harsh, inhuman face of life. This however forged his character and made him a good man, filled with love. The privations he experienced were great but the will to stand on his feet and learn how to read and write was greater still.

So life recompensed him even if he had to go through many turbulent years. Reaching the height of social and professional distinction, he didn't forget what he had been through.

As we wrote just now life was not always good to Mr Tranoúlis. From when he was a child he was obliged to go into the deep waters of the struggle to survive. He had hardly time to learn to play and to read and write before he learned to earn his daily wage in a furnace. Panayótis Tranoúlis was born in Aíghio into a large family of seven children! At the age of seven he was left fatherless and replaced him in the furnace where his father had worked.

A barbarous moulder was to cripple him on the left arm hitting him with a fearsome stick. But little Panayótis would continue to work without the "luxury" of going to school. At the age of ten with a will, you would think, of granite, he decided to teach himself how to read and write. As he himself characteristically says: "I knew no greater joy than this." After work, he applied himself avidly to reading, many times at the expense of his rest and sleep. He could let his stomach be empty of food but filled his brain with learning and his heart with the happiness of knowledge.

At the age of seventeen his first poem was published in the journal "Bouquet". There followed acquaintance with important people in Greek letters (Stélios Anemodourás, Vasílis Rótas, Voúla Damianákou, Galáteia Kazantzáki, etc.) who gave him favourable reviews.

Then followed his occupational achievements with the creation of his own business which was expanding all the time. The business was no other than that which he had under his skin from childhood, a furnace that produced bricks. Afterwards came marriage and the creation of a family with two children. Later came his other four "children" the books which he wrote. Their titles are: "Keratohóri", "For a Grape", "From Furnace to Prison", and "In Hiding". All four were enthusiastically received by the critics and the public alike. They have also been translated into Russian and Hungarian.

The vigorous and realistic style has been compared with that of Maxim Gorky.

His universal messages and his humanity which flows from his books brings to mind another giant of world literature, also a child of the Mediterranean, the Frenchman Jean Genet.

The restless mind of Panayótis Tranoúlis didn't stop there. The Intellectual Centre, which bears his name, was created at Pikérmi and every year it awards a prize for the best novel, so passing on his love of literature . . .

This year too the Centre's prize will be awarded to the best writer of the year . . .

May the example of Mr Tranoúlis be followed by others with the same zeal and altruism.

Denis Tzannátos

MIHALIS MERAKLIS, University Professor, Folklorist
7-31-1981

My dear Mr Tranoúlis

The fact that I didn't reply when I received your new book (a sequel to the previous one) puzzled you, as I understand, and you sent it to me again by registered post.

I'm sorry I gave you this trouble.

I beg you to understand my failure to reply. The modern intellectual is sometimes equally alienated, subjugated by (apart from other things) temporal pressures and hardships, to the point where he too feels tragic, like the unskilled, hardworking man of your childhood years, as is narrated in your excellent and perhaps from one point of view, unique books which comprise a kind of proletarian ethology, that will be more broadly discussed.

Yours faithfully

ALEXANDRA DELIGHEORGHI, University Professor
9-29-1973

Dear Mr Tranoúlis

It is almost a month since I read your book. In this letter

I want to thank you and congratulate you for the invaluable work you have done in writing this book.

As far as I know we haven't any works that analyse, even within the limits of sociology, the period, with its harsh conditions, that is unfolded in your book. I wish to thank you with all my heart, not only because you cover a sociological gap, recording from first hand experience the poverty of an epoch which we could quite easily forget, even though it still concerns us, but chiefly because you achieve something like that in the field of literature where situations stay fast in the memory and take root better in the consciousness. I was deeply impressed by the immediacy and pure power that characterize your writing. Personally I consider your book to be a precious literary and sociological document. And I think that literature can count on few such soul-stirring documents that do not betray it.

I've heard from my mother that you intend to write, as a sequel to the first, two more books. So my letter gives me particularly the opportunity to wish you well in your new endeavour, because it doesn't escape me how much effort is needed to bring a trilogy to fruition like the one in which you want to complete "Keratohóri". May the honour of having your book prefaced by Vasílis Rótas and the thought that people will read it who will be genuinely moved, becoming better aware that the social struggle in harsh conditions means the struggle for survival and humanisation, give you all the strength needed.

YANNIS KOFINIS, Novelist-Poet 8-23-1987

My dear Mr Panayótis

I was lucky that I didn't leave Pendéli—I suffered a heat-stroke and I stayed almost six hours wrapped in ice, in a state of aphasia, and with a temperature of 105 until the moment they conveyed me to the Hospital where I saw your great social works, and came into contact with you again with the delivery of "Review". Why was I losing you? With how much pleasure I recall your visits to the little farm at Pendéli. Your greatness lies in the fact that you are open-hearted, a truly good man, and for that reason a real and outstanding writer. Your experience of the arrest in the furnace is described in some of the most beautiful pages in our literature to present that sad epoch and I say frankly just as I have written it to you, it is the most genuine and amazing description. Now I have your address and I send you my two last books.

With love

Yánnis Kofínis

MIHALIS STAFYLAS 10-17-1980

Brother Panayótis, Gorky of our time.

Beyond what I shall write about your book I want to shake your hand and congratulate you. It's the first time I've read a book (yours) without stopping. It's not only plain, working-class literature; it's a bitter history of the working-class when the workers were under the absolute control of their boss.

Your book is the book of the year. I believe it will be an injustice if it doesn't get the First State Prize for Prose because it is written with sweat and blood, with suffering, and with love for your fellow-being.

Dear Panayótis, I don't think that there exists a more delightful and full book. I'll write this in a special essay because the "Grape" is in a class of its own in our literature.

I kiss you and congratulate you.

Mihális Stafylás

YANNIS HATZINIS, Novelist-Critic 5-1-1973, Journal "Néa Estía"

As I read "Keratohóri", memories close in on me from all sides. First and foremost from my former reading of Panaït Istráti, Hamsun, and Maxim Gorky who exploited in an excellent creative way the autobiographical in their books. Perhaps even from some American writers who revealed to us an almost unbelievable misery. But more so from my own memories of childhood years in a village in the Ighemonías district on the island of Samos where the children came to school barefoot (it's doubtful if one in ten wore shoes) shivering with cold when their father wasn't occupying them in the fields, the furnaces, and at the fishing. I remember them at break-time hovering around the confectioner's tray with the lollipops and not having the five lepta needed to taste them. It was the time when every Sunday the butcher slaughtered a billy goat for a village of four thousand inhabitants.

My mind goes back to what was happening there around 1900 every summer when I take refuge in the village to relax and escape the exhaust fumes. But nobody remembers those things because the village is now rich since every family has two or three seamen working on the boats. It's another story whether these sailors are the new martyrs with the dangerous and harsh life they live so that their families can have a good life. Mr Tranoúlis will excuse me for saying this but I think that one must have personal understanding to be a good reader of a book like "Keratohóri".

From the moment I took up the book I didn't raise my head until I had reached the end. The book is short but it would have been the same if it had been double or triple the size. It is in fact an "essay" (as Vasílis Rótas and Voúla Damianákou characterize it in their joint prefatory note), an essay which takes the form of a work of literature, thanks to the plain style, the timely detection of the necessary, and the understated dramatisation that govern the pen of Mr Tranoúlis.

It is a chronicle like those written sometimes without a sequel, for the purpose of recounting a situation in a tragic tone in order to draw attention to a tragedy. Therefore it isn't important whether or not Mr Tranoúlis continues writing. It is enough that he has presented his testimony which is not to be hidden deep in some archive, but to be read, and, if it is possible, to wake some consciences from lethargy. I don't know if in our country such villages continue to exist where life is lived at the ultimate limits of corruption, exploitation, and wretchedness.

But we now live in a world that has shrunk so much that

it is confined as if within the boundaries of the former small village. And the misery of Vietnam, for example, can awake in us the same reactions, even more intense, more shocking when we see that the so-called "Greats" (to whatever camp they belong) are only playing on a large scale, the role of the boss in "Keratohóri" who is interested most of all in his brick furnaces and the higher production that will fill his pockets with thousand drachma notes, rather than in the unfortunate workers who produce the bricks.

Mr Tranoúlis, essentially, reminds us that we live in a wretched world, corrupt and blind. His snapshots, that give us a vivid picture of extreme wretchedness in a small village could, for whoever has some imagination, take on such a dimension as would embrace the entire world of man.

THE LIFE OF
PANAYÓTIS TRANOÚLIS

Panayótis Tranoúlis was born in Aíghio in a family of seven other children, in a little one room house belonging to the boss of the tile furnace where his father worked.

When he was two years old he was brought to Athens. They lived in a poor neighbourhood further down from Rouf barracks.

When he was seven his father died, and instead of going to school, he was brought to work in the furnace where his parent had worked. At that age, a moulder hit him on the shoulder with a heavy stick called a "strike" and left him crippled for the rest of his life.

In winter, when the furnaces closed down, he worked in tanneries. He cleaned cisterns in freezing water above his knees, cisterns that stank horribly—at that time skins were lubricated with dogs' excrement—in small tannery works, with burning soda and potash, he scraped cisterns three or four metres deep and when he was slow in coming up for a breath of air, so as he could do as much work as possible, his nose ran with blood.

He did many other jobs.

In a few years they found themselves in Peristéri in a refugee hut.

At the age of ten or eleven he saw that he wouldn't be able to go to school and began to teach himself to read and write. On Sundays, he would gather the children of the first class in his house with their readers and he would learn with them.

He was eager to learn. He was composing verses in his head and wanted to write them down so as not to forget them . . .

He gave himself completely to studying. He said that he knew no greater happiness than that. The hours he didn't have work he spent reading and writing. In the evenings he would read and sometimes, when he stopped to go to bed, he saw that it was already dawn . . . He didn't care that he was leaving for work, not having slept. He would sing.

He felt happy, rich within himself because he had learned such great things! It was as if he were living a perpetual feast-day.

What did it matter if very often he didn't have bread, not even for a snack!

When he learned that the vowels were seven and the consonants seventeen, he was brimming over with joy; he used to say he was so happy his feet scarcely touched the ground.

In 1929 they exchanged huts and went to Néa Sfagheía near his work.

As he grew up, his life changed for the better.

He kept company with young people who were educated. Some of them published poems and short stories. When he was seventeen or eighteen, he sent a poem to the journal "Bouquet". They published it in the back pages, in the commentary section and they wrote: "The poem loses in musical rhythm." Underneath, they had even put some musical notes!

On Thursdays he would go to Kallithéa to Élli Alexíou's literary evenings. There he met many writers such as Menélaos Loudémis, Galáteia Kazantzáki, and others.

Tranoúlis, a little worker from the furnace, made them warm to him because he was learning by heart poems by foreigners, as well as by Greek poets. Once they requested him to recite a section from Goethe's "Faust". When he finished, Galáteia Kazantzáki got up, kissed him and said: "*I* don't even know one quatrain from 'Faust'!"

From that moment he had her respect. He would recite poems by Alexander Puskin, Paul Verlaine, Baudelaine, Schiller, Edgar Alan Poe, Victor Hugo, Heinrich Heine, and others.

He knew "Faust" almost by heart. His great admiration for the work of Goethe made him want to write a "Faust" too. He filled notebooks with poems. During the 1940's war the notebooks were scattered, together with his false dreams, as he used to say.

But he didn't stop reading.

He studied the Greek classics, Homer, Sophocles, Aeschylus, Euriphides, Plato, Plutarch, Xenophon, as well as modern poets, Palamás, Várnalis, Kaváfy etc.

He met and became friends with the writers Stélios Anemodourás, Yórghos Kotzioúlas, Stávros Tsakínis, Grighóris Yerásimos, Yánnis Skarímbas, Vasílis Rótas, Voúla Damianákou, Nikifóros Vrettákos, Yánnis Rítsos etc.

In 1950 he set up a small business, a brick furnace at Rafína. Gradually he expanded it.

In 1953 he got married. In 1954 his first son was born, followed in one and a half years, by a second son. From the first class in primary school to their final year at high school he helped his sons with grammar, history, mathematics, and all their other subjects which he himself read first. He did the same with unfamiliar words. He looked them up in dictionaries, especially the "Proía[1] Modern World Encyclopaedia".

In 1973 he wrote his first book "Keratohóri" with a foreword by Vasílis Rótas and Voúla Damianákou, which surprised the literary circles.

Tranoúlis used to go down often with Vasílis Rótas and Voúla Damianákou to Gytheion and the villages around, to relax. One time at Scoutári by the sea Tranoúlis read them extracts from his writings. When he finished Vasílis Rótas got up, shook him by the hand and said: "Congratulations. From this moment I consider you my intellectual brother. You must compile a book from these and I'll write you a preface." Voúla Damianákou also got up, shook his hand and said: "I'll write you a preface too." Tranoúlis used to say that if it hadn't been for Rótas and Damianákou his book would not perhaps have been published. He said that he learned a lot from being with them. They stirred his enthusiasm for literature.

In 1980 he wrote his second book, "For a Grape" and in 1981 the third, "From Furnace to Prison".

In 1983 his briefcase with a collection of short stories about the working-class, ready for printing, was stolen from his car.

In 1989 he produced his fourth book of short stories

---

[1]Proía is the trade name for the encyclopaedia.

under the title "In Hiding".

When his first book was published, critical reviews appeared. Rótas said: "No one knows what kind of book this is. It is a poem. An ancient tragedy."

Tranoúlis's books received almost three hundred commentaries in letters, journals, and newspapers that placed him in the first rank of the great writers of world literature. He himself certainly didn't agree with this.

In 1983 his book "Keratohóri" was read by the actor Kóstas Kazákos in fourteen episodes on the Athens National Radio arts programme.

Also his books "Keratohóri", "For a Grape", and "From Furnace to Prison" were translated in 1993 into Russian by the prestigious publishing house "Rándouka" in Moscow.

In 2001 his book "Keratohóri" was translated into Hungarian by the University of Budapest, and in 2004 into Spanish by the University of Venezuela.

In 1984 at Aghía Paraskeví, 505 Mesogheíon Street Panayótis Tranoúlis founded, under official statute, the Cultural Centre that bears his name.

From that time until 2000 the Centre awarded two prizes for literature and two for the arts every year.

From 2001 it has been awarding prizes only for the novel, by Greek or foreign writers, thus giving the prize an international dimension.

Panayótis Tranoúlis today lives in Palaiá Pendéli with his wife, his two sons, one a doctor and the other an architect, his two daughters-in-law, both scientists, and his four grandchildren.

ABOUT THE TRANSLATOR

Marjorie Chambers was born in Northern Ireland and educated at Trinity College, Dublin and the Sorbonne. For many years she taught Modern Greek Language and Literature at Queen's University, Belfast. Her translations of Greek poetry, prose, and drama have been published in the USA, Greece, England, and Ireland. The poets and writers she has translated include: Yánnis Rítsos, Nikifóros Vrettákos, George Vafópoulos, Níkos Gátsos, Míltos Sahtoúris, Iákovos Kampanéllis, Christóforos Miliónis, and Yánnis Kondós.